This wise, poignant, closely observed book opens a window into the world of dementia. People with this condition lose many things, but as Scott shows with sensitivity and grace, they never lose the need for warm, loving human contact, *and frequently give it.*

> Michael Castleman, Co-author:
> *There's Still a Person In There: The Complete Guide to Preventing, Treating, and Coping with Alzheimer's Disease* (Putnam, 1999)

*A Joyful Encounter...*is a tender glimpse into a fragile world where we might find ourselves later in life. Lynn Scott's poetic narrative leaves me with a new understanding of the human spirit reaching out to heal present relationships—and those we thought we'd lost forever.

> Teresa LeYung Ryan, Author
> *Love Made of Heart,* (Kensington Books, 2002)

A Joyful Encounter

Oct, 2017

Here's reading for your journey
to Chicago —
and my wishes for the
trip to be perfect —
It wasn't my karma so long
ago to have you in my life
But it is now, & I am
most grateful!

with love, Lynn

A Joyful Encounter

✦

My Mother, My Alzheimer Clients, and Me

A Memoir by Lynn Scott

iUniverse, Inc.
New York Lincoln Shanghai

A Joyful Encounter
My Mother, My Alzheimer Clients, and Me

Copyright © 2005 by Lynn Scott

iUniverse books may be ordered through booksellers or by contacting:

iUniverse
2021 Pine Lake Road, Suite 100
Lincoln, NE 68512
www.iuniverse.com
1-800-Authors (1-800-288-4677)

ISBN-13: 978-0-595-36211-0 (pbk)
ISBN-13: 978-0-595-80655-3 (ebk)
ISBN-10: 0-595-36211-7 (pbk)
ISBN-10: 0-595-80655-4 (ebk)

Printed in the United States of America

MY HEART ACKNOWLEDGES

Shane Snowden, good friend through so many life changes, who, this year, topped her many material gifts to me by bringing this book into the light.

Marie Ryan Pappas, gentle friend and excellent spiritual advisor, who lovingly opened me to deeper insights in my writing.

My San Francisco groups and their leaders, George Birimisa and Suze Allen, and editors Ruth Wynkoop and Adele Horwitz, whose excellent critiquing enabled me to come to some measure of what constitutes good writing.

My current critique group, Teresa LeYung Ryan, Judith Marshall, and Naomi Marcia Berger, writers all—we four—such a fine team.

The supportive literary world of the Bay Area California Writers Club and its members, especially, Linda Joy Myers, Teresa LeYung Ryan, Elisa Southard.

My longtime friends who have sustained me materially, emotionally, and professionally through our long journey together.

My family of children and Grandchildren—the bliss and the tears

DEDICATION

For Mebs and Marietta,
and the hundreds of thousands of people who,
despite loss of conversation, can still give love
served with irony, humor, tenderness, and vulnerability.
And in recognition of the Spirit that is within each of us,
one continuous flow from life through death and ever after.

At last to be identified
At last, the lamps upon thy side
The rest of life to see!

Emily Dickinson
Resurgam

Contents

Introduction

I needed money. I was sixty-seven and living thinly on Social Security. I sent out notices to upscale home associations, thinking I might be paid to travel with an older person as companion. I was offered only one job. I took it. Instead of voyages to foreign lands, I began caretaking Marietta, midway through her journey with Alzheimer's disease. I had no idea I would find myself on a personal sojourn of my own.

Marietta had been losing her memory and compensating in frustrating ways over a long period of time. In the tenth year of her decline, her desperate husband, Hank, hired me to be her overnight companion. I have had a succession of older women mentors throughout my life, wise women who accepted me as I was whenever we met. I had never had a mentor/mother like Marietta.

After I gave one-on-one care to Marietta for over a year in her home, her family moved her to an Alzheimer facility that I'll call Homeport. A job opened there for an Activities Director. With no previous experience in keeping this population alert and interested, I jumped in. My education expanded under the improbable tutelage of each member of Marietta's new "family" in that unit. I began to re-examine the attitudes and beliefs I had held about my mother, Mebs, who had died in dementia twenty years before. Working intimately with my clients at Homeport, no longer as a reactive child, but as an adult of the same age my mother was when she died, I gradually developed as much tenderness and compassion for her life as I had now for Marietta.

It takes courage and gallantry to grow old without bitterness, even when all one's past is erased. I have been touched by the Spirit within each body, despite its weight of a flawed mind. Spirit rises out of pain, loss, and sadness, rosy-tinged with tenderness and giggles. I experienced it all.

"I Can Hear The Music Of The Song Of Love I Sang With You"

Always In My Heart

San Francisco, 1998

Marietta is at the door of her elegant family home, wearing one of her perennial leisure suits, when I enter with my key. I've been her caregiver for three weeks. "Oh it's you, Mary, how nice to see you."

She pushes out a nervous chuckle that startles because her face shows no expression. Her coarse hair, a hennaed brown, and her stiff stance make her seem wooden. Her brown eyes wear a cloudy scrim, like glass curtains protecting the insider from the curious. Her initial formality is of long habit, but I will soon put her at ease. My name is Lynn, but to Marietta I am one of her two "Marys," taking over from Mary #1 five afternoons a week. I carry my overnight bag to the bedroom near hers.

"I'm staying over tonight, and we're going to have fun!" I say.

"You'll be with me tonight? Oh good, you know I don't like being alone."

The loneliness is bottomless. How must it be to lose the moment just before this one—and only this second to be *here*, before *here* is lost forever? Where does one dwell when there is no memory of the immediate past?

Yet Marietta remembers me each time. Her intuition is intact. I find it easy to tell her over and over that I will stay with her, that her husband will return. I don't mistake her for her illness. She is still there behind the ancient stone-goddess mask that has replaced her dark good looks. Pictures of this former beauty are arrayed on her grand piano: The athlete on the tennis court; galloping across a beach on horseback beside her husband, Hank; sitting by a swimming pool with her young child, Susan.

"Ready for some tennis?" I say now.

"Tennis? Oh yes," she speaks with some energy, "I love to play. Where is my racquet?"

2

When she could no longer remember the rules in doubles games with her husband, I picked up a racquet, for the first time in forty-five years, to replace him. My father's attempts to make a tennis player out of me had been foiled by my tendency to faint in the hot East Coast summer sun. But here, in cool San Francisco, Marietta and I have played on public courts all over the city. Marietta takes her place in one spot of the court, saying over and over, as my shots sail wildly across the net, "No, Mary. Not over there—*to me, to me here!*"

What a good teacher! By this edict I am forced to learn control, focus, delivery to where she waits with her easy athlete's return. And because every yesterday has dropped into a black void, she is the perfect partner for me, thrilled each day to get back to the courts, forgetting how inept a player I really am.

I was delighted to find that Marietta played the piano, and musicals were her specialty. Music had been the one soothing element throughout my childhood that had bound my family together. On our vacation car trips throughout the East Coast during the '30s and '40s, we sang. My mother, Mebs, would carry the tune in her deep alto, Dad harmonized in a high tenor, and my brother and I, well into our teens, sang along without embarrassment. We learned all the words of those songs written before we were born, when blues songs defined women's roles:

> *What's the difference if I say I'll go away*
> *when I know that I'll be back on my knees one day.*

Marietta and I sit together on the piano bench while she plays and we sing show tunes going back to the 'twenties. We are "girls", only three years apart, and bonded now by the enduring songs from musicals—words planted in our memories, even Marietta's, even now.

We are delighted when we finish together in some harmony. In a bad imitation of Audrey Hepburn, I keep singing "I could have dahnced all night…" I pull Marietta up to dance.

"Oh Mary," she says, reduced to giggles, "you always make me laugh!"

Marietta reminded me of Mebs in her denial of the shadows in her life. Mebs drank. Marietta sang, snatches of song, when someone hurt her. I have watched her cover feelings behind a quick humming tune, always the same one with words that end "…and more than that, I wish you love."

Husband Hank descends from his sanctum on the floor above, heading out for the evening. "Where are you going dear?"

"Out to dinner. I'll see you in the morning."

"Can't I come with you?" No whining, just a question.

"No, not tonight. Enjoy dinner with Lynn." And he is gone. She hums "...I wish you love."

Much later, seated beside me in front of the television, the feeling is still with her. She asks me, "Wouldn't you think he could take me out with him sometimes? Perhaps he has found someone else."

I am speechless, because of course he has. Ten years of endings have taken a toll on Hank too. He has moved on. She cannot grasp why. No one has told her. The family's inability to speak of this tragedy leaves her with a deep sense of guilt, believing that she makes mistakes, fails them in some way.

"Mary, I want to go home, can you help me?"

"Look around you, Marietta. These are your things, this is the house you and Hank so beautifully decorated, raised your child in, entertained in."

But I know it is something else she is after: A sense of personal power and purpose. Taking a big risk, I decide to break through the silence of this family.

"I know you are lonely, Marietta." I tell her about the loss of memory, how it affects her, and her family. "It is a cross you have to bear." I speak the language of the Church of her upbringing and education. I know of her abiding trust in a benevolent God. "None of it is your fault. You know God is always with you."

She listens closely, no humming now. She asks me questions. "My parents are gone, aren't they? But where is my sister? Why can't I live with her?"

I tell her honestly that her sister just isn't available, never comes west to see her. That is another cross for her to bear. She nods. She knows this already, somewhere in the cells of her body. It isn't new, just freshly stated between us.

"I can remember when I lived with my parents, and I remember Susan when she was little."

"Yes, you certainly do. You've just lost your short-term memory. For instance, can you remember what we had for supper?"

She admits the blank with a shake of her head. She is thinking hard. Finally she reaches out and takes my hand, "Thank you Mary." She is looking at me with love—no scrim before her eyes now. "I am so happy you are with me, telling me these things."

"I'll tell you each time you feel lonely," I say. I am suddenly husky-voiced. I reach in my bag and pull out a Hershey bar.

"Oh, Mary, I love chocolate!"

We watch television in a comfortable chocolate silence.

"From Now On There'll Be A Change In Me"

There'll Be Some Changes Made

Marietta's escape from family in Chicago has a mystery to it. Her daughter once alluded to a first marriage. Perhaps it was then that Marietta was set free from the pressures of a rigid Catholic family life where her German father ruled with an iron hand. He bought her a car when she was twenty-two, not to find her own pleasure, but to take her mother shopping. I have seen pictures of Marietta's mother through the years. She was beautiful, but around her hung the shadow of another unseen, undervalued woman. She wasn't present—eyes looking inward, an isolate, surrounded by husband, daughter Marietta, and Marietta's sister and brother.

Marietta would go on about that family, especially where they met around the dinner table. While Marietta talked lovingly, I imagined a depressed mother, a bullying father, and three held down children. Marietta believed all the furniture around her was from that home. This would infuriate her husband, Hank, who had worked hard to outdo his arrogant father-in-law, and had succeeded in his various enterprises.

Whoever took Marietta to California, he didn't remain on the scene long. I love that my ladylike, subservient Marietta did not run back home. She did office work until she met Hank. She was an avid sportswoman and met him at her tennis club. I am sure her father made Hank's life miserable. He was from a poor immigrant background, Jewish, and had not yet proven himself in the work world.

He still bore that humiliation all these years later, evident when he straightened me out about the things in their house—all *his* accumulations, nothing to do with Marietta's father.

My mother, Mebs, was the child of Lutheran missionaries who founded an orphan home in Fort Lee, New Jersey. Any cash my grandparents accumulated

5

went to the orphans. Mebs and her two sisters never took part in the American dream. She never overcame her early experiences of second-hand clothes, or the lack of girlish luxuries, festooning herself in large costume jewelry, and putting great emphasis on personal appearance all her adult life. She married my father, George, a womanizer, who paid no attention to finances, leaving Mebs to worry over the bills and to maintain the illusion of a middle class life. Like Marietta, she was both over-protected and undervalued. She leaked out her feelings without discussion, and these indirect calls for help set me into a lifelong role as problem solver when I was often inadequate to the task.

"Feel Like Dancing Down The Street"

Broadway Rhythm

Marietta and I roamed across San Francisco for over a year, two unlikely vagabonds seeking every tennis court open to the city's denizens; finding easy paths through the Presidio woods; walking its bay shore from the boat basin to Fort Point where we snooped through the old guardian fort at the golden gate. When her long athlete's stride exhausted me, we visited neighborhoods, stopping frequently for our favorite treat, chocolate ice cream. I tried museums, but Marietta wasn't big on looking at static things.

Marietta's conversation then was fairly repetitive and often centered on her original family, her beautiful mother, her father's edicts. Each time we passed the local Catholic girls' school, she would tell me that was her school. Actually her daughter had attended this school with the same name as Marietta's Chicago high school.

I frequently escorted Marietta to Sunday Mass at her familiar church. The service was modern and lovely, and, to my joy, Marietta knew all the words in the responses. My heart swelled as she joined the other parishioners and became whole during that ancient litany. We reached another level in those high experiences. Words simply weren't important.

When Hank went out in the evening, she could sound quite angry to see him drive off in the Mercedes, believing it was the original car her father had given her. She seemed to resent his driving "her car," or did her mind hold the knowledge that she was cast off? It was the only time she showed anger toward Hank.

After our amazing talk about her problem, I felt easy about reminding her when she began her anxious requests to "go home." Sometimes that worked; other times, if a candy bar or singing together didn't distract her, I would call her sister or her brother in Chicago. She would tell them of her wish to come home and they would be hard put to explain why they never visited her.

We ate the meals Hank often prepared, and worked together to clean up the kitchen. Here is where I saw the perfectionist side of Marietta that affected her daughter as she was growing to adulthood. If I hung the pots "backwards" or didn't replace the china just where it had been, she would "tsk tsk" and put things right. The lady of the house was still very present. Of course, Hank told me that he made the meals whenever their housekeeper had a day off. Marietta had never learned to cook, probably had never used a vacuum, nevertheless, knew where things belonged.

As the year progressed, Marietta grew more unwilling to take baths, get her hair washed, or change her clothes. Luckily, the other "Mary" took care of the first two issues. Being the night person, I had the job of getting Marietta out of her leisure suit and into her nightgown. She was very modest so I set things out and left her alone. Eventually, I would find her tucked into bed, fully dressed. Sometimes I would get her up and explain, as I began undressing her, how it wasn't sanitary to wear her day clothes under the covers. I thought this might appeal to her sense of rightness, and sometimes it did. But if she was just plain determined, I would shrug, let her go back to bed, and hang her nightgown back in the closet. I learned to let go of concepts that simply made no sense to Marietta.

Homeport
"No, You're Not The Same"

When Marietta's husband and daughter could no longer cope with their loss of Marietta's mind, its frustrations and constancy, they placed her in a brand new facility that included an Alzheimer unit I call Homeport. After my initial reaction against her being moved from her home, my hopes rose that she would be happier with constant company about her. When one cannot go inward to commune peacefully, the community becomes especially important. Marietta was initially put in a room-share with Kate (alias Capt. Queeg). I found her there on a drop-in visit.

Homeport is on the bottom floor of a four-story senior complex a city block long. Unlike the nursing home where Mebs ended up, the floors are carpeted, and the sitting areas look like a living room in any upper middle class home. Only by touching the printed fabrics can you see that they are as easily maintained as the dull hospital chairs I sat in with my mother years before. The other difference—no smells. Who can ever forget the mixed odors of urine and disinfectant that grow like poison flowers in most nursing homes? At Homeport, no one is sitting around in wheel chairs for hours without care. It was a revelation to me after my limited experience.

When I came to visit Marietta, she greeted me in her warm ladylike way. Her familiar things: a bank of framed photographs on the deep window sill; a bureau from her bedroom full of the little things she'd saved, like broken costume jewelry and combs and lipsticks; a single bed with the familiar bedspread I had smoothed so often, were contained in one side of a medium-sized room. But the room was closed down—blinds and windows shut. I switched on a light, and heard a growl from Kate's direction where she sat staring off into the gloom, her clothes a jumble on her almost prostrate body.

"*Turn out those lights!*" I jumped to obey, then quickly escorted Marietta out of there to the small sitting room within this suite of five bedrooms. She asked the familiar question, "Mary can you take me home?" Soon the wisdom of the administration was to move her to an empty room where for a few months she lived by herself. She didn't do well alone. There was far too much isolation within her mind to take pleasure in outer solitude. Again, on my visits, she would anxiously ask, "Can't you bring me home, Mary? I am sure I can live with my sister."

I was moved to tears at her loneliness, and, in extension, to my mother's. What went on in Mebs' mind? She never spoke to me as deeply as Marietta did. The pain of imagining her thoughts, however fractured, and her unspoken feelings, made me reach out to Marietta like a daughter, happily free of any mother/daughter history.

"Just As Long As We're Together"

Marietta's rescue from too much solitude came in the form of Eileen, a sister substitute who became her roommate. Marietta settled in. Eileen had been a librarian, but it appears, from a picture she has on her bedside table, her prime achievement was as ballroom dancer. It is an elegant picture—a far younger and fuller Eileen swung wide by her partner, smiling like a star in a made-for-dancing dress with layers of ruffled underskirts. I would bring the picture out when there was someone new to show it to, and, while Eileen would disparage it, I could see beneath this ruse, her delight in being center stage for another brief moment.

Eileen still wears her bright white hair in a longish pageboy, and, with a touch of lipstick is gauntly beautiful. Her records say she is in her eighties, ten years older than Marietta, but her childlike dependence and eagerness to please make her seem the younger sister. I catch signs of her wily ways, her hidden strength beneath the 'girly' presentation. Eileen has never been without a man. She took Marietta's arm on that first day and never let go again. Marietta no longer talks of being alone. They are Castor and Pollux, Ruth and Naomi, yoked, matched, bracketed, and, in Eileen's eyes at least, man and woman.

"Where is he, I've lost him. Where *is* he?" she asks me.

"Marietta went out to lunch with her husband. She'll be back."

She pouts, mumbles angrily about the person who has stolen her love. What a formidable competitor she must have been. I doubt she lost her men to anyone.

Marietta rarely makes an issue of her changed gender. After all, in her eyes, Eileen is always 'Mary' to Marietta, and Eileen doesn't complain either. But Marietta's daughter, Susan, wanting some time alone with her mother, is angrily vocal in front of Eileen, "She calls my mother 'he' I hate that!"

Am I alone in seeing Eileen pull inside, try to disappear, still clinging to Marietta's hand? I tell the daughter, "What good luck for your mom! She has been missing her sister for years and now she has one. Isn't that true, Marietta?"

"Yes, I suppose so."

11

Marietta's disease, or maybe it is the small amount of medication she is on, doesn't allow for a range of emotion. It is this equanimity and her warm politeness that even the most angrily unbalanced resident cannot attack. Everyone likes Marietta. I believe everyone always did. Like Mebs, she combines a ladylike vulnerability with an almost voyeuristic attention to the stories others tell her. And, like Marietta, Mebs placed a high emphasis on social propriety.

Marietta's husband, Hank, had an upscale restaurant for a number of years. He told me, "Marietta was the hostess. Dressed elegantly to match the decor, she would move around the tables greeting people, witty yet ladylike, never intruding. She made the place," he said.

"Though I See The Danger There"

Fools Rush In

I had expressed interest in a part time job at Homeport when I made my visits and met the Director. She and I had been back and forth for weeks. She first asked me to be an aide on the night shift. Staying awake "in case" was not something I felt I could honor—my body/mind would undermine my duty by nodding off, leaving the wandering patients endangered. As we dickered, the full-time Activities Director gave notice. The Director offered me the job. As much as I wanted to work with Marietta and the others whom I was getting to know on my visits, I was determined to keep most of my week for writing. I suggested I share the week with the other part timer until a full time person could be found. The Homeport Director and I met with the Executive Director who had the additional responsibility for the one hundred seniors living in apartments on the floors above. I felt the pull from each side—their competition for my availability. Since I hardly knew what the job consisted of, it made me nervous. Finally, they agreed that I would spend most of my two or three days a week in Homeport but go upstairs to do morning chair exercises, lead the bi-weekly bingo games, and, eventually, try a writing/book reading group.

I never had an orientation for this job. The exiting full time person talked to me for ten minutes, telling me where to find equipment. The other part-time person claimed illness a week after I began. I think she found the pressure to cover the whole building too frightening. I only had three days to follow her around before she left. I learned how she did the exercises, but not much more. I was blind to what was ahead.

Shelves had never been put up in the activities room closets. I found games (many not appropriate for my clientele), sports equipment, song sheets in a pile together. My first weeks were spent organizing suitable and available resources, all the while holding groups together with music and word games that my clients would know. I had to learn names, read histories, dash upstairs for my duties there, and research possible additions to our limited supplies. There was no budget for buying new things. All requests had to go through the head administration—an endless and often fruitless project.

As the numbers of clients grew and more Homeport suites opened up, I wore a path up and down that vast football field of a building, from the activities room out to the lobby and up the stairs—a superannuated quarterback struggling to hold onto an unfamiliar ball, with no team in sight. I think, had not Marietta been here, so pleased to have me around, I might have taken that ball to a touchdown—out to the lobby, down to my car, and *gone!* But my boss, the Homeport Director, was a patient listener, and tried to help me make sense of things.

Homeport is an airless space. I am a fresh oxygen freak. The saving grace of Homeport is its three courtyards, landscaped with a circle of grass and flowers in the center, where I can just manage a circle of chairs. I take as many of my activities outside as often as possible, luring the Homeporters out with the promise of hats and snacks, and singing in the sun. The courtyards are bounded on three sides by our building, and on the fourth side we look at blank windows in neighboring apartments. No one, even the upstairs residents with a view to this green space, poke their heads out to say hello, urge us on in our simple outdoor sports of badminton, golf putts, ball tossing, or to join us in song. Homeport is a thing to be feared: Loss of yet another home upstairs and being moved behind locked doors. Most of those folks avoid us as they would a leper colony.

I learn on the job how to keep the growing group of clients, all with different levels of dementia, interested, alert, and active. I give physical energy, my heart, and my imagination, using all of the skills from my past as counselor and group facilitator, and, to my delight, those songs of my past. Without realizing it at first, I have this chance to redo those last years with my mother. Now I see this must have been the source of much of my seeming fearlessness in taking on such a difficult job.

Life Among Marietta's New Family
"I've Got A Smile On My Face"

Singing in the Rain

Whenever I can't think of a thing to do, at least once a day, I gather a group on one of the patios, pass out the song sheets, and cool out with an hour of singing. If anyone tires of this activity they never object. Music holds the center, draws each person out, calms the agitated, unites disparate backgrounds if the songs have been national favorites over the years. Any person can sing. It doesn't matter how people sing, even off-key, because it has the effect of smoothing neural pathways, and aligning the subtle vibrations of the body.

At Homeport, Marietta and I are delighted to continue our singing. Early on she stopped trying to keep up on the piano, but our familiar songs are still in our minds. I hand out the song sheets and begin on page one. My a cappella has a pure pitch, at least visitors tell me so. I can't believe how many tunes I carry in my brain. Soon everyone joins in, even restless Bill or medication-driven Arnold. It is the one activity that will engage every Homeporter. Soon we become a group, not a set of disparate desperates.

Everyone is tolerant of the atonals and speedy or slow singers, and only a few raise eyebrows as Arnold ends each song in a high falsetto. I remind them all of Tiny Tim. He was a success in high tones.

Occasionally, I simply can't get off on the right note. Then I turn to one or another Homeporter. At least one will get the pitch and off we go. It interests me that music, old and familiar tunes and words, is always reachable in my clients. We sing beneath the circle of apartments above us. I wonder what the feelings are beyond the open windows above. If my belief about the commonality of song holds true, they are humming and healing too.

15

Sophie says good-naturedly, "I don't need the song sheet, I know the words to every song." And, as the songs take me back to my childhood, I believe each one of them still can envision a different time and different place.

I know that I envision my mother and myself in the back seat, my brother driving with Dad beside him, while we sing old songs for miles of vacation roads.

"Pack Up Your Troubles In Your Old Kit Bag"

Taking on the job at Homeport, adding other teachers in the form of Marietta's new "family," led to my heart opening still further to my mother, Mebs. I didn't know I would find wisdom in the wit and wise comments emerging from the damaged minds of my clients. It was as if Spirit found direct pathways to touch me through the lacunae of their brains. I was developing a state of grace in which my wounded child within was accepting Mebs and holding her with the love and tenderness I felt for my clients.

At 92, Sophie isn't in Homeport so much for dementia as plain tiredness, and a body that requires a walker and someone to follow after her. She is likely to forget her limitations and fling herself into an upright position from a chair and march off, on an angle. I drop into her room in the morning to cajole her into joining the exercise and discussion group. We talk.

"My mother was very active—here is her picture." I look at a middle-aged woman, small, perky, with red hair and a serious demeanor.

"Sophie, she looks just like you."

"Yes, and so does my daughter."

"And was your mother an activist too?" She nods.

"Three generations of women who were hardly your run-of-the-mill housewives. Your daughter tells me you went back to school in middle age and became a social worker."

"I lost my young son in a trolley accident, then my husband died as a young man. What else was I to do?"

"I guess it wouldn't even have occurred to you to be depressed for the rest of your life and do nothing." This came from the adult child of Mebs whose depression affected my childhood so profoundly.

"No way!" Sophie definitely hadn't used that route.

Sophie is not an exacting judge. She watches without contempt as Bob pounds tabletops, Arnold interrupts gatherings. She goes back to studying the paper, one page for an hour. She is serene within herself.

This morning her daughter, an outgoing forthright reminder of what Sophie used to be, stops by to see Sophie as I am reading aloud items from today's newspaper. She has brought a neighborhood paper in which she has an article that she wrote about the threatened closing of one of the two hospitals that serve the poor of the city. I ask her to explain to the group. She is a good talker. This is a vacation for me.

Finishing up that subject, with a small touch to her mother's shoulder she says, "Do you know my mother founded Friends of the Park? And," she adds, "mother is still known for raising funds so poor children can attend concerts and ballet." Sophie says nothing and looks embarrassed. What she did was simply who she was—a person who gave for the love of it, expecting no rewards.

I am imagining myself at Sophie's age, always delighted by new ideas. And suddenly I am thinking of Mebs. How different we always were. She was a youthful beauty with a self-disparagement like Marietta's roommate, Eileen, and, like Marietta, she wore innocence like a cape she would wrap her denial in if she could not face a fact. I, more like Sophie and her daughter, imagined I had a more realistic view of events going on around me. The fact that I had put up with my philandering husband for years, suffering diminishing self-esteem, and never pushed for a real conversation with Mebs, seemed to elude forthright me.

I was a constant thorn in my mother's side. I remember her telling me to "be more like your sister-in-law, play bridge, be social, be more selfish." Be more selfish! I was appalled. Not only did that sort of social life bore me, but also, I had long before taken my life philosophy from Nana and Papa, Mebs' immigrant Norwegian parents. Nana and Papa's environment, where I spent much of my childhood, was Jesus-centered. We sang, not popular songs, but hymns and children's chants: *"Jesus loves me this I know, for the Bible tells me so."* After each meal we picked Biblical sayings from a little black box kept on the table. I adored this ritual. Add to it the fierce love and down home cooking, soul food that filled in the chinks of my lonesome heart.

It is poignant to think how different was my mother's experience as a child of this devout household. Where she found unrelenting piety, I found light and joy. I didn't know then that Mebs' childhood, albeit based on love, denied her some little thing to call her own, so she felt similar to the orphans her parents rescued. As if to make up for her childhood deprivations, she wore rings with very large semi-precious stones, and her ear lobes stretched from the huge earrings that bedecked them. In contrast, I wore no jewelry, but for an occasional bracelet.

Sophie's daughter looks around at the Homeport group members, half of whom are dozing. "Well, I see I've put people to sleep. I'd better stop now."

I say, "Oh, please, don't take it personally. This is par for the course. I've had to learn that. Even upstairs, in the middle of my exciting book review, half the group dozes off. I hope it gets in by osmosis. It's lovely hearing your news, being read to."

But she moves off to the other side of the living room to talk with the wife of a new man in our unit. I wish she would come each time a new family enters, help them adjust. I am always drawn to tell family members how they can stretch past old beliefs about dementia to the remaining irony, humor, alert comment that boosts my days in Homeport to spiritual heights. Too late for my mother, but not for these new teachers of mine to be seen more deeply by family members.

Conversation isn't all. Each individual I work with sends out sparks of life, which keep me from writing off all they still must be feeling. Think of the deep sadness of being torn from all you have known and plopped among "strangers" often without being told of your illness, which adds to your fear that it is something you have done that caused you to be cast out. The litany strings out from each Homeporter on different days in different forms and I respond individually to each one. Sometimes humor works, or agreement, or an honest correction.

"Where is my home, when will I return?" "This is your new home. Isn't it nice never being alone, having things to do all day."

"I have a dog, have you seen him?" "No, but will you show me his picture?"

"Do you like cats? I always have at least one cat." "I love cats, and you have yours with you, let's go to your room and I'll brush her."

"Will you take me out in my car. It's in my garage." "Bill, your wife has your car and often takes you out riding in it. She'll be here today."

"My oldest friend (or my father or mother) is coming today. I want the place to look nice. I will serve tea. Do we have some cake?"

"Yes, everything will be ready."

Added to all of the above, is the invariable blackness that causes each to forget that earlier this day a visitor *has* been here to see them.

"He's Just My Bill, An Ordinary Guy"

Just Plain Bill

A piercing fingers-under-the-tongue whistle tells me, a room away, that Bill, the former advertising man, is up. He is getting to be a later and later sleeper. Bill's a man's man: fishing, golf, cocktails, constant social activity. There are mostly women in Homeport, and the few men aren't of Bill's ilk. He cannot understand the loss of his circle, the abandonment he feels. He wants to know where his car is, his wife, his life.

"What are we doing? Where's Phyllis (his wife)?"

He hates the group exercises, physical or mental. His face begins to scrunch up, he pounds his fist against the table or chair arm, and in a low desperate voice he curses, says loudly "this is all crap," speaking to no one in particular.

"I'm dying!" That topic, combined with his angry tone, makes some of the women nervous. A man's anger, where might it lead?

If I am not in the middle of a program, I say "Let's take a walk, Bill. Let's go see if the fountain is on." I take his arm, stroll with him. Because Bill reminds me of the men who peopled my parents' living room and the endless cocktail party guests on my in-laws summer porch, I have a relaxed dialogue with him.

Scratching his back, strolling arm in arm with him up and down the halls and courtyards, talking about his life, highlighting the talks with easy teasing or slightly ribald remarks, make us both believe in his wholeness. He is so familiar. On the surface a self-reliant charmer, but in truth, aslant against the wife who holds up the whole structure from which he does his man thing.

The Welsh poet, Dylan Thomas, would have liked drinking with Bill. Like Thomas' father, Bill may be dying. Unlike Mr. Thomas, he certainly is "raging, raging against the dying of the light." On this day, once again, I try to explain about Homeport, about his memory loss and how his wife never abandons him. He listens, has trouble believing it, but settles down. After the walk I find him a snack. Food is a comfort. And now, bed rest. I lead him to his room where he throws himself, stomach down, across his bed sideways, shoes dangling away from the spread. His mother's admonitions still remembered?

As I turn, I see his memoir on the bureau, the one he wrote just at the beginning of the memory loss so there would be a record of his life. We look at it together sometimes. He's had a rich life, a privileged life, in which he was socially adept, accomplished, unheeding of a future he would never have dreamed.

Once I asked his wife, "Where are all Bill's golfing buddies? How come no one visits him?" Her answer saddened me. "I've discouraged them from coming. He can't hold a conversation."

But he can still joke, see humor in things. One day as I walked past his lunch table I heard him mutter, "Wow, what a big guy!" I wiggled my hips at him and said, "These ain't no guy hips, Bill, look again."

"Oh *really!*" he said, his grin as it must have been among the guys when the jokes began. He would recognize his friends' humor at least. Are we only friends for as long as a conversation can happen?

Each time Phyllis comes, he brightens, seems almost the man he always expected to be. She gives him his blue sea captain's cap and they stroll out for a ride in that car he so often asks about, never back to his home, too hard on the heart, but out to the world that goes on without him.

"Some Others I've Seen...Might Never Be Cross, Try To Be Boss"

Stubbornness is a trait society disparages. It is a constant at Homeport. In this setting, stubbornness is the last ditch effort to hang onto the Self. With the loss of short-term memory, unfamiliar surroundings, forgotten family and friends, one only has the things around her and her own body. On this day, we've had our morning snack, cut up fruit and a drink of juice. One of the aides has left a small paring knife on the fruit tray and I see Naomi wrap it up in her napkin. I know better than to approach her directly. She is a saver. Perhaps she always was, but how understandable that now, reduced to one room, among strangers, she hangs onto everything she picks up. It can be a music sheet she won't relinquish at the end of our singing, or her plate of fruit that she wraps untouched.

A knife is more serious, but diversion is the best route. How often, when my kids were small, I didn't take the time to notice what involved them in that moment when I asked them to do something. I would spout impatiently, cause a blow-up, and make us both feel badly. Perhaps it is because these are adults, and old, that I respect their needs to hang onto what makes them unique, and use diversionary tactics. I show Naomi a picture book, ask her to hold it for me. She needs two hands, puts down the knife, and takes the book. I remove the knife without her seeing me.

Naomi cannot be hustled onto the next activity. She sits stolidly, and if urged, will say, "I am not going to do that now, maybe later."

I quickly learn diplomacy with this crowd. I may ask for help. "Naomi, you know those wonderful ditties. I hope you will help me remember the words. We are meeting right in the next room. Can I help you out of that chair?" Sometimes that works, but often I tell her about a project, walk away, and a while later an aide will bring her pleasantly into the group.

Penelope, a thin spinster, married to one job all her work life, is a romantic. As with so many long-lived romantics, she has a well-developed cynicism. "I live among crazies" she has muttered during a meal as Bill, alone at his table for two, yells for ice cream. Yet, I have sometimes lured her for an art project or mind games from her overheated single room, comfortably full of a life's collection of furniture and books. I feel her isolation, see her shyness, and her grudging gratitude when asked to be a part of the community.

There are a few for whom I have a struggle with my judgment. Esther, humorless and anxious, cannot be lured into the group, cannot give up her constant refrain. She asks, in her broad New York dialect, everyone who passes, "Where is my daughter?"

I come to understand that my reaction to Esther is brought about by my seeing her aging daughter's loss of self; see, in her resignation, a pattern of demand and response set for a lifetime, familiarly like my own, and even more like my mother's. At first I tease Esther, saying with her, "Where is my daughter?" before she gets the words out. She is rarely able to enjoy the entertainment by outside groups. "Where is my daughter?" she will say loudly while an entertainer sings over her endless litany.

Certainly Esther's anxiety is typical—and very understandable. If I don't stop projecting my inner resentments onto Esther, I am as stuck as she. That is far too narrow a path to tread for long. I work to get her included in the sing-along or the mind quizzes, and when she slips into her rut I tell her once again that her daughter will return in the afternoon, a promise. Each of these breakouts I make from my long-held resentments releases pieces of my heart, sealed for so much of my life.

"I Love You Truly, Truly Dear"

I Love You Truly

Caroline, hair blonded and neatly coifed, wears a bright pink dress suit. She is still pretty at eightysome. She looks like an upper class matron as she leans toward you. But she speaks only gibberish now. It is importantly spoken. I wonder if she knows inside what she is trying to say. Some definitely know they aren't getting the right words out.

Most of her peers smile at her, even try to understand what she is saying if she should sit beside them, unless her brain has moved into some moonscape where rage exists. Then they move away, frightened. Aides take her with caution since they have been punched and scratched at different times. She can turn suddenly paranoid and angry.

Now she rises from a chair and begins to pull it after her. Her face, bruised by frequent falls when she gets up in the night without help, looks frighteningly scowly.

"This is my brother's chair. You aren't going to have it. I am taking it home, get out of my way."

"Caroline, I saw another of his chairs in the wrong place. Let me show you."

By the time she gets to her room she has forgotten the chair and is led to the next activity. Lately she is better on new medication, and, amazingly, lives peacefully in a room with Naomi, silent and unobtrusive, a former therapist.

Caroline has one daughter, a professional woman, who comes in daily. The daughter bends toward the mother, stroking her face, talking to her as if they are in dialogue. I feel the pang of loss that such moments did not occur between Mebs and me. Then I let it go. The love that transcends the quirky moods of a damaged mind is palpable. My heart swells to it. The human spirit can be coaxed out, even now, even in me.

"You, You're Driving Me Crazy. What Did I Do, What Did I Do?"

For at least three months, Kate, Marietta's first roommate, sat in her darkened room and would not move. One day I noticed that she was eating in her suite dining room, albeit alone at a table. That was a first. I began greeting her each day, telling her what we were about to do and inviting her to come. She refused, but smiled.

Kate's commanding voice comes right off a hog-calling farm, or, as it turns out, was the tone she used as a naval officer long ago. Since the kitchen server has to bring food from the far dining area, across the end of the living room to Kate's table, when Kate wants something, she shouts commands across that space, demanding soup, or a napkin, or dessert.

Recently Bill was placed across from her at the table for two in the suite where the food is served. On this day Bill has his food in front of him but is asking for dessert. Several of the aides and I have urged him to eat his meal then dessert will soon be coming. "Oh goody" says he, and doesn't eat. Soon he begins again to ask for ice cream.

"Eat your lunch and stop bothering everyone." Kate's voice booms out and Bill stops in his tracks.

"Wow, you sound like my sergeant in the army!" He's impressed.

"Well you're wrong. I was a Lieutenant in the Navy. Now quiet down."

The aides smile at the unexpected help and plan to keep those two together for every meal.

Months later Kate has opened out. Her depression has lifted. She still demurs at my exercise offer in the morning, but she is walking well and is often in the small living room off her room. Her son plans to move her soon to a smaller facility. She is the only Homeporter who is better off than when she arrived. I'm glad no one here will realize her absence. But then, do I really know that?

"A Wider World Of Joy I See Because You Come To Me"

Because

There is no typical day in Homeport. Families of the clients come and go all during the day; the wellness people come in to take blood pressure, check on anyone with a complaint; the aides drop in and out of my groups with meds for individuals, or to rub cream on skin blemishes. They speak in their own language from one room to another. They carry dirty laundry past us and start up the washing machine hidden behind doors at the end of the living room.

Maintenance people come clanking through with tools to fix the endless breaks in the system, for instance, emergency doors that begin humming, scaring the staff into taking a head count to see that no Homeporter has left the premises. The food servers are constantly busy passing my groups with rattling servers on which are clattering dishes and silver for the next meal. There are mid-morning and mid-afternoon snacks to distribute to the assembled. At any time of day representatives of the administration may bring potential clients or inspectors. I never saw such activity at my mother's last residence. I never found her out of her bed, being entertained, unless a family member was visiting.

The aides in Homeport, mostly Filipinas, maintain a generous spirit in the face of low salaries, no breaks, constant clean-ups, and uniquely difficult personalities. Aside from all they must do to maintain the clients and the units, they are asked to substitute for me when I go upstairs among the independent living apartments to lead exercise, call a bingo game, or do a weekly book review.

None get a break. My work with the patients is fun very often. It is hard for the aides to take the time to see the uniqueness of each person they are serving. Yet new aides soon soften their edges, their too-swift movements, because the tempo of Homeport revolves around the patients with all their human needs and personalities. Most of the aides bring this empathy to their work with their clients. These individual women from all classes of Filipino society work to earn a living, or a green card, or full citizenship. For instance, Kara's husband is a proto-

26

col officer in Italy for the Philippine government. They visit one another every several months.

I ask, "Wouldn't you have servants as his wife in Italy?"

"Yes, but I stay to become a U.S. citizen."

Though citizenship is her priority, something I have always taken for granted, I warm to her way of loving these folks we tend. She is ever so gentle and respect-ful even to those who occasionally become violent. And sometimes, despite how busy she is, she will take time alone with a client. One day, shortly after Isaac had arrived, nervous and disoriented, I was looking for Kara. I finally found her in Isaac's room, sitting like an honored guest, listening as he played his viola. I crept back out, not wanting to disturb the important bonding that was going on. Later she found me, her eyes bright with tears.

"I cannot describe the feeling—it was like being made love to with music."

And we continue to receive amid all our giving.

"Woman Needs Man And Man Must Have His Mate"

Isaac, the complex musician, he who holds the holocaust against his chest like a suit of daggers pointing in, plays the Don Juan game as if the outer side of his chest plate advertises, "the secret to life is Romance."

I meet him coming out of his room. His eyes light up with a satyr's glow.

"What you up to?" I ask.

"Mischief!"

"What brand?"

"Any I can find—right side up or up side down."

But there is the deeper love he still holds for his former wife. She hasn't abandoned him. She and their daughter visit frequently and he is considered part of her new family. Most of the time he is placid about her remarriage, but he has spoken in one-liners about being "odd man out." She dropped in this morning while we were in our exercise group and they went off to his room for an hour or so, where she helps him with his finances, listens to his concerns about the music world of which he sometimes believes he is still a part.

Later, as I am rushing toward the door to go upstairs for my weekly book review, he calls to me, catches up, tells me something wonderful has happened. I would tell him to wait till later but there is no teasing in his eyes. They are shining as though he has seen a vision.

"What has happened?" I ask, smiling.

"I told my ex-wife I loved her. She told me she loves me too."

"I am basking in your joy," I say, stopping for a good hug.

"We Made A Blunder...I Wonder If You're Blue Too"

Working together by chance one Saturday recently, Mark, the new fulltime activities leader, and I note a disturbing change in Arnold. His wife has dropped him off a bit later than usual from their quarters upstairs in the regular senior apartments. Normally, Arnold is one of our easier clients. He occasionally resents being dropped with us while his wife goes about her business, but soon melds in blandly. He was an accountant and if he gets mad at anyone he repeats over and over that they won't see the two million he's made.

He enters most days doing his extra-loud finger snapping all the way down the corridor. "I am The Snapper," he declares, and we all agree he wins, fingers down. But not today. His wife sees him to a chair beside me at the table where the group is gathered for the morning news. Then she leaves. Mark is reading quotes from a book called *The Meaning of Life*. Arnold speaks out. "My missus had twelve strong drinks!" He repeats this until Mark focuses on him.

"How are you feeling about that Arnold?"

"I hate it. I am going to tell Harold. He'll fix her."

"You do that, Arnold. Will you listen to this reading? It may help." Mark continues.

"She told everyone I have Alzheimer's—I *don't* have Alzheimer's!"

I touch his arm, "You really are angry about that aren't you?"

"You're damned right...and she had twelve strong drinks!"

He is growing more agitated, repeating the two phrases over and over. I put my arm on his shoulder. Mark asks him not to interrupt till he finishes what he is reading. Arnold stands suddenly, begins to laugh.

"I can say the whole alphabet backwards" and off he goes. Mark puts his book down resignedly.

I flash back to when I must have been no older than eight. Desperate for attention from my distracted mother, I copied out a poem from my beloved

Book House Books, tore out the page and ripped it into shreds, and took my copy to Mebs for appreciation. Hardly glancing at it, she said "that's nice dear, go write some more," and turned away. Even being exposed as a poem thief would have been better than not being seen at all. I felt the same desperateness in Arnold.

Arnold is a flawless backwards alphabet reciter. When he is done he laughs and snaps his fingers. Mark says, "Arnold, we can talk later. Right now we are going to do some chair exercises. Let's turn our chairs into a circle."

Arnold mutters that his wife had all those drinks and told everyone he has Alzheimer's. He gets up. Mark, rather forcefully, asks him to sit down. Arnold begins to cry. Mark apologizes, comes round, and leads Arnold off for a talk. Our goal is not to squelch any attempt at individuality as long as it hurts no one. Arnold's dignity has been sorely wounded. He needs an outlet for his feelings.

I lead the group in exercise. Marietta, who used to work her athlete's body, now barely moves arms or legs, but she loves to count. She keeps the timing, always counting to twelve. I tease her when the exercise is to count on our fingers.

"What! You have twelve fingers, Marietta? Let's see them."

Mark comes back with Arnold who seems calmer. Mark begins a game of balloon tossing within the circle. Arnold heads for the dining room. We've had the morning snack and it is a half hour till lunch. I hear an aide scold him for taking a banana. That would have been a good time for me to lure him back. But I bat the balloon and let the moment pass.

After lunch and some down time, the group is gathered again. I am trying a new exercise, poetry writing. I start with the word 'green.'

"What do you think of when you see the word 'green?'" A list is begun: grass, leaves, caterpillar, velvet.

Arnold pops up. "I wrote a song." He sings it to a little tune he's made up.

"That's lovely Arnold, really lovely. You are a poet. Can you help us with this poem? What is the feeling when you think of grass?"

"My song is about peach of mind…" And once again he sings.

I already feel nervous with Mark present and this untried exercise moving like a snail through molasses. I only have two lines written out: 'Caterpillars transforming, butterflies blooming'. Arnold begins again with his song. I give up my plan.

"Okay, Arnold. Go slowly. I'm going to write the whole thing down." I have him repeat it until it is there, below my two lines.

"In the search of peach of mind
We should love all humankind
And our love will grow to be
For us a joy forever.
We will feel happiness
That will grow everywhere.
Peach of mind for you and me
And all loving families.
Then the whole world will be dearer
As we grow nearer
To having peach of mind."

I let go of my plan—choosing a little 'peach' for myself.

On Sunday I'm alone with the group. Arnold is there and back into his mantra, "My missus had twelve drinks and I'm going to report her. She told everyone I have Alzheimer's."

I can't leave the group for one-on-one time with Arnold. He won't sit and I soon hear the aides yelling about disappearing bananas. It seems he makes a tour of all the suites, helping himself to at least four bananas. Since several of the clients, more deeply in advanced stages of brain loss, do wander across boundaries, there are now hook and eye latches inside the bottom of the Dutch doors to each bedroom, but somehow they aren't secured against Arnold on this day.

Time slides by. A visiting aide on her way out, signals that I'd better check the side dining room. The group is singing now. I slip off and, as I enter the door, there is Arnold, bent over behind a table, pants down, about to release a final statement in his rage.

"No, Arnold, this is the dining room, not the bathroom. Let me take you there."

"Leave me alone!" He begins pushing it out.

I yell for the aide who rushes in, tries to take his arm. He almost hits her. She is frightened and goes to the phone to call his wife. I return to the group, wanting them to all stay together, not discover the brewing disaster. Arnold's wife arrives, and soon he is led out, pants up and intact. Just then the maintenance man arrives with scrubbing equipment and I know Arnold has succeeded in delivering his strongest message.

I keep us singing. I hear the water vacuum going in the dining room, and see, approaching us down the long corridor from the entrance, the Homeport Director in tow with a potential client. They go into the newest suite, open now with only four clients, and I fervently wish that they hold the visitor's attention until the cleaner is finished.

The group sings on. I introduce each song and the year it came out, and who in this group likes it especially, keep my eye on any move to disband, and send vibes to the Director not to come this way soon. We are in luck. Enough time elapses for the maintenance person to be in the last stage of the clean up. As a matter of fact, his presence is probably a good indication to the visitor of our attention to cleanliness. It is a large step upward from my mother's nursing facility. Most of the clients think they are in a residential hotel with room service and meals. And so it appears.

"*Then, Like My Dreams, They Fade And Die*"

I've gathered a few folks in the room with the grand piano. I had hoped that Marietta would continue to play and we would sing to her accompaniment, but she had no one urging her to it those first months at Homeport and now, with the disease gobbling up her brain, she cannot play at all.

But this is a special grand piano, a technological wonder. Just push a button, a chip is activated, and a full-blown concert begins, albeit a bit thin toned. We sit listening while the keys move as if a virtuoso *eminence grise* has slid onto the piano bench.

Marietta's husband, Hank, in for his faithful visit, finds us there and nods silently as he takes his place beside her. She takes his hand. Eileen, on her left, begins her usual fidgeting and dirty looks.

For months now, I have been promising to give Marietta's family a copy of my memoir about our time together in that first year while she still lived at home. Now it is in printed form and I have brought him a copy. I am a bit frightened. How will he take it? I reveal that I had known about his new relationship back then, though he had never told me personally. And I have focussed just on Marietta's pain—not on his or his daughter's.

I hand it to him silently while the music tinkles on around us. I sit across from him and surreptitiously glance often to see his reaction. Do I see him wipe away a tear? I hold my breath as he finishes and closes the little booklet. He *is* crying and looking at me with love and gratitude. I go over.

"It is just beautiful," he says.

And I know his tears are for the woman he lost who sits beside him now, smiling, taking his hand, and loving him still.

"We Tripped The Light Fantastic"

The weather is take-a-walk beautiful. Some of the Homeporters can do a block, even two. It is the organization to get us all out there that takes immeasurable time. Bill needs his cap. Naomi needs a sweater. Eileen always needs her walking shoes, which she never puts on first thing in the morning, choosing always her dainty heels. It is another of those annoyances that I discover has much to do with Mebs' pressure on me to "be a lady, be more feminine."

As I run to get each thing, the little gathered group begins de-forming like the oil bubbles in those mesmerizing lava lamps. So I am a herding sheep dog in between my dives into closets.

Estelle is always ready for a real walk. She is a short person who looks tall in her tight chignon, dyed a deep black, and her well-kept body, tanned by her daily bask in the sun on one of the patios. She is elegant in black slacks and top, over which is a sweater the pale lavender of a first gladiola on its long stalk. Even her dark cane with the onyx head looks classy. It is no wonder on this day, while she waits under the sidewalk canopy for the gang to assemble, that a passing young man blurts out, "You sure look elegant." She is first startled then very pleased. I've overheard and give her a thumbs-up.

Marietta in her ubiquitous leisure suit and good walking shoes, ready to step into her athletic gait, has Eileen on her arm. Eileen, ever the girly girl in skirt, stockings, still has on her ridiculous Minnie Mouse shoes that she steps out of frequently if she lifts up her feet to walk. *Damn!* I forgot to bring her walking shoes. Now her little girl/old woman mincing steps will slow Marietta down. Marietta might tell her to move faster or she might just accept the pace. I encourage Eileen to step out, big steps, like Marietta. She does this while I am looking, but quickly reverts to the mincing steps. I think of the dancer she was, and I'm sad for her.

The line gets going. I hold Bill's arm, then the "girl duo" and, slipping farther behind, are Estelle and Isaac, a companionable pair of about the same pace and

34

conversational level. I stop and wait for them at each corner, much to the impatience of both Bill and Marietta, "Let's go, the light is green!" In this hurry-along-and-wait way we make it around the building. I point out each person's room, jutting out above us, trying to give them a place to belong to.

A place to belong to…I am remembering my mother and me taking walks. We would go out after dark in our suburban neighborhood. I must have been between twelve and fourteen in those years. Did we hold hands? I'd like to believe so. Our aim was to see how others lived, what the house decor was like. We were just plain nosy. We didn't like it at all if the shades were pulled. We gave those houses an F. It was fun, and quite harmless.

Here, now, walking with folks whose homes might not even be memories, I wonder what goes on in the minds of the drivers waiting for us to cross in front of them. Do they see us at all? Do they understand each of us has a history/herstory? Women past a certain age are quite invisible on the street. I know that from experience. If the motorists see us, are we quickly written off as "decrepits" whose life is over? Until I took up this work I would not see the individuals in such a group, just note if they were disabled in some way, feel a bit of pity, drive on. There's nothing like walking in others' moccasins to view life from a different perspective.

"Hail! Hail! The Gang's All Here, What The Heck Do We Care Now?"

Hail! Hail! The Gang's All Here

I often feel badly that Homeport has no references to the Chinese culture Lotus is from. During one sing-along I asked her and her ubiquitous attendant to sing a childhood song in her own dialect. They did. And we clapped. Small compensation. I made it my business to learn her Chinese name and pronunciation. At least, each day when I greet her with this name, she feels seen, and rewards me with a big smile. I have to work to get her into the circle for the daily morning exercises. She is anxious until her attendant comes. I point to a chair facing the corridor to the main entrance.

"You will see her as soon as she comes, and she will see you," I say.

As my mother and I drove along in my teens, we had an exercise routine. We'd scrunch up our faces, then open our mouths wide, stretching them into a rictus grin over and over. This was a Jack LaLanne exercise my mother used to protect against a double chin. We wouldn't look left or right, hoping people in cars passing us or walking on the sidewalk would do a double take.

I introduced this exercise to my group. "Eyes and mouth wide open, then scrunch everything up, push out your lips." Lotus and I began to make the face at each other. She would sometimes seem afraid of my face. (Who knew what were her experiences with "white devils" in long ago Hong Kong?) I would look afraid at her face. Now it is a part of our routine. When I'm passing her, especially when her caregiver is with her and she feels safe, I make the face and she makes one back. And we giggle.

We have sing-along hymns, distinctly Christian in text. Naomi's son brought in a packet of Yiddish songs, but only the full time activities leader knew Yiddish. Since almost everyone knows the popular songs of yesteryear, we sing these most often.

The true caste system in Homeport is really about where one is on the scale toward dementia. Despite what outsiders think of the Homeport group, it is not homogeneous in this. Those with some memory loss but still very present, (though rarely loquacious) tend to band together around the two-or four-person tables at mealtime. They roll their eyes when Bill agonizes publicly or Arnold the Snapper roams among them like a lost boy.

Among them, a few respond favorably to a discussion of ideas, hungry to put out their often emotion-laden thoughts. Isaac, for instance, formerly a violist who bordered on the edge of fame, holds the whole Nazi catastrophe on his face in repose. He claims he is an atheist, but he is nevertheless furious at a God that would let millions of people die, let a Hitler rise!

I suggest, "Maybe there is no big man in the sky manipulating this world, raining down terror."

"What then is our purpose?" he responds angrily, belying his atheism.

"For whatever reason, maybe we are here to learn there is no separation between us."

"Why a Hitler then? What possible use is a Hitler?"

"I don't know. He certainly focussed on separation! Someone once told me that "sin" came from a Greek word in archery meaning missing the mark. Perhaps we're meant to catch and help those troubled children before they get to be Hitlers."

But Isaac cannot get past the deaths—"nine million Jews!"

"And another several million gypsies, homosexuals, handicapped, and even German nationals," I add.

We don't come to solutions or conclusions, but the exercise is good. Isaac is stimulated, alert. He thanks me for the discussion, which has gone on for ten minutes over the heads of the others in the group who listen without comment. And I am, as usual, forced to look my spiritual values in the eye, those from my childhood with my Norwegian grandparents, and those I have added from my spiritual seeking—clarifying, clarifying forever.

"Put On Your Old Gray Bonnet With The Blue Ribbon On It"

Put On Your Old Gray Bonnet

I've got seven or eight of the Homeporters sitting together on the benches in the sun. We could be mistaken for boardwalk sitters in Southern California. Some are wearing the various hats from the collection kept on the rack in the living room just for these occasions. Two are in straw cowboy hats. Eileen always wants the fuchsia felt that matches most of her clothes. Marietta needs a large one and will take any that fit. Sophie won't wear one despite her white skin and her daughter's admonitions.

"I've always sat in the sun. I am fine!" Period, end of report.

Bill watches, his sea captain's cap covering his tender baldpate. If I don't get going quickly he will ask, "What's happening?" and rise and stroll off. I sit across from "my pupils" on a rolling chair I've brought from inside, like a teacher, ready to test their brainpower.

"Okay, here are the first lines of some treasured poems. Can you quote the next lines? 'Once upon a midnight dreary...'"

Sophie picks it up without a pause: "As I pondered, weak and weary—Poe."

"Well okay Sophie. Here's another: 'The hand that rocks the cradle...'"

"Rules the world...but I doubt that is true." Sophie again.

This is worth discussing.

"Did everyone hear what Sophie said? She doubts it is true that mothers really rule the world. What do you think?" I look at Bill first.

"Mother took good care of us," he muses.

"I loved my little girl." Marietta's warm brown eyes seem to be looking into a scene from her past.

"Did you feel you ruled the world as a mother?"

"Oh, I wouldn't say that...My father would say 'Marietta, take your mother out shopping today.' My mother was lovely, so beautiful."

Eileen talks mistily, "My mother made all my dresses. She was so good to me."

I've noticed that when I attempt to get a discussion going among most seniors in their eighties and above, mothers are always good, generous, lovely. Fathers sometimes too, but often they aren't mentioned or haven't left a strong imprint. So perhaps, in that sense, mothers do land on top, at least in the wishful memories of those late in years.

After several more first lines that Sophie immediately continues, the group is looking with respect at her command of poetry. I direct an easy one toward Marietta. She will know the second line of any popular song from the twenties to the forties.

"Here's a poem made into a song, Marietta, 'I think that I shall never see…'"

She sings, "A poem lovely as a tree."

"Right on! And Naomi, here's a ditty I bet you know: 'Father calls me William, Sister calls me Will, Mother calls me Willie…" She is already saying it with me and continues, "But the fellers call me Bill."

We giggle together. Then, without a pause, she intones, "The little old maid took a bath. She didn't tell a soul. Forgot to put the stopper in, and went right down the hole." Naomi pantomimes the circling water, the old maid disappearing. I laugh out loud. I love that her mind, so often stuck in silence, retains snatches of song and ditties so full of irony.

"I'd Like To Leave It All Behind"

Let the Rest of the World Go By

Half the kitchen staff walked out last night, leaving the overworked aides to serve breakfast and clear tables. I helped them with lunch. There was one great moment. I approached Marietta, Eileen, and Naomi sitting together at a table.

"How are you ladies doing?" I ask.

Naomi snaps, "We're doing everyone who allows us to!"

Events in this place, those that cause anxiety, have a way of hanging in the air like fly paper. The Homeporters note changes. Some are less demanding, others more anxious. Lately the events have been especially heavy: Penelope off to the hospital with a uterine infection. Will she get back, or is she gone from her home-like room forever? Bill and Caroline have taken falls. He wears a bandage over the lumpy stitches on his head. She sports a neon-red cheek. A new aide administered the wrong medication to Kate who took the mix-up most generously.

These events are reported to the state watchdog agency. At what point will it judge this place unsafe? I am torn. I don't want to see this unit closed down, for my sake, and certainly so my clients are not disrupted. Yet the for-profit company is stinting on help and salaries. My activist-for-the-underdog self wants to see things improve for everyone.

All this is on my mind at the end of the day as I gather everyone from the three suites into a circle of chairs in the living room. We have a treat ahead. Isaac's daughter, a mezzo-soprano, has come to sing for the group with a new friend, a soprano—a divine coupling. Singing excerpts from Stabat Mater, the two voices, both light and richly textured, are so harmonically sympathetic that they waft me into that inner place one can sometimes reach at the heart of the music. At the end I look around at each Homeporter. Not one is asleep. All clap. Most smile. The music has reached where they are still whole.

"You Hold Her Hand And She Holds Yours, And That's A Very Good Sign"

The group is gathered in the recreation room doing an art project with the weekly art teacher. Each one has a paintbrush and is assiduously painting little wooden mosaic chips as the first stage of some grand scheme the teacher has in mind. Their last project floats over their heads—a huge mobile hung with colorfully collaged paper plates.

Now it is time to clean up. I hand out wet towels. Some easily wipe off the water-based paint, but Eileen and Marietta are having difficulty. I take Eileen's hands first and wipe hard at the paint stuck onto her red nail polish.

"Oooo, that hurts, you're pinching." She pulls her hand away, all the time smiling at me. I apologize, stop for a minute to be present, more gentle. Then I get the job done.

"Thank you, thank you, you're so wonderful." She fawns, makes nice. And I wonder again what her life was like that caused her this frequent self-abashment.

I gently wipe Marietta's hands. She is meticulous. It took some coaxing to get her to paint at all. There was no way to do the job without touching the paint. As I finish she looks up at me and in her ladylike way, smiles and says thank you. And then, her usually opaque brown eyes full with feeling, she says, "I love you."

I say, "I love you too." How easy. I feel those hollow places within me drop away. Marietta, apparently a difficult mother, unknowingly gives me the opportunity to accept a mother's love and to reply with gentle touch.

Lessons, lessons! Here I thought I was doing arts and crafts with my clients, when the lesson was mine. When I do not tune into the unique personality I am working with there will be a reaction. Can't each of us feel that time in our growing up when we acted out, or we buried ourselves inside, when someone did not

41

see our essence? All of the staff has to learn that, or suffer the consequences, in which case, patients to suffer too.

Going roughshod over Eileen's sensitive fingers reminded me of how frequently I did that with my children as they were growing. I see my grown children now being so respectful of their children's different natures. I see what a difference it makes for peaceful and loving interactions.

"We Will Dance The Hoochee Koochee"

Meet Me In St. Louis

A lazy afternoon…got to wake everyone up…get bodies moving, alert. I put on a great Big Band tape, all Marietta's and my old favorites: Dorsey and Goodman and Whiteman, "Pennsylvania Station," "Chattanooga Choo Choo," "Sentimental Journey."

"Okay, who's up for dancing?"

I know I can count on Marietta and Eileen. Isaac, with that satyr's twinkle in his eye, is heading for me. "Let's dance close," he twinkles suggestively, the old roué still alive and well—at least in Isaac's brain.

"You wild man!" I feed his ego, why not? It pushes into the background that terribly sad part of him.

I dance a bit with him then lead him toward Estelle, who won't get up to dance unless he charms her. She leaves her cane by her chair and, elegant as usual, rises to the occasion. I pull Lotus up, away from her attendant, teasing, cajoling, and saying I know she was a dancer back in Hong Kong. She is seduced, tells me, as we sway, that she had many boyfriends there, danced all the time. Ah, accessible memories evoke smiles and bring lightness to each of these dear people. Lotus' attendant cuts in and I move around the circle to Sophie behind her walker.

"Let's cut a rug, Soph," I say, shoving aside the walker and getting her on her feet. I am holding both her hands, trying to keep the touch light but ready to catch her if she leans too far over. At ninety-two she is a second generation San Franciscan.

"Did you dance in this city when you were young?" I ask.

"Years ago there were dances and dancing classes. I did it all."

She tires quickly and I seat her again. I move to Naomi, past Arnold who stands snapping his fingers to the beat. Naomi, often so shut down, has a beautiful smile, and it is there now. I pick up her hands, and she comes. We dance, or,

43

as with everyone, we shuffle or sway. It looks like a party. And, perfectly, here comes the Director with yet another potential client.

I think how differently we try to do things here than in the nursing homes I have unhappily visited. My mother never wanted to go to one. I never wanted her to either. Yet, that is where she ended up. I never saw her in a group activity. How I would have loved to find my mother dancing.

"And Try To Find The Sunny Side Of Life"

It is late in the afternoon. The folks are dispersed. Some to their rooms for a rest, a few sitting around the living room table listening to music, one or two in their suite in front of the television. Only Bill is moving. His family tends to come near the end of the day and he is restless. "Scratch my back please." It is a simple intimate act I can do. Then I invite him outside to stroll the circle of the courtyard in the sun. We sit on a bench.

"Your family will show, Bill. They always do. They are faithful. You have nice children."

"Yes, I do."

"Shows you did something right, gave them respect."

"Yes, I guess I did."

"If a grandchild came to you and asked for advice for living, what would you say?" (A very brief pause) *"Love Life!"* Clear and most ingenuous from a guy who knows he has lost his.

"What better thing could you say! And I do believe you always have."

"Yes, I always have loved life."

On another day, a few of us sitting together, and I ask Sophie this question. She says in her usual no nonsense way, "You've got to live it!"

From my left Estelle says, "Yes, and you're lucky to have it!"

I say, "So what risks have you taken in your lives?" Silence. Then Sophie, whom I thought was dozing by now, raises her head, looks me in the eye and says, "We're taking a chance every morning just getting up." Ah so.

"For Tis Love And Love Alone The World Is Seeking"

Times and traditions mark a person's age as much as their looks. I can't imagine what the baby boomers' generation, or my technology-focussed grandchildren's generation will be like as they move into senior and special care facilities. The generation in Homeport, those in their late seventies to mid-nineties, had experienced, despite two world wars and the prejudices of society, cohesive family and community values that had, at base, graciousness in relating to other individuals. Called simply, "manners,'" it runs deeper than a societal need to keep order. It respects, both physically and verbally, another human's self-circumscription.

I know to approach Sophie, asleep in her chair, newspaper folded as if she is reading, with a gentle voice so I don't startle her. She is a bit deaf, and if I touch her, she jumps. But no matter how she is wakened, I can count on a smile of respect when she recognizes me. Even grouchy Penelope, after I carefully knock at her closed door and try to draw her out to some activity, covers her resistance with starchy humor that doesn't leave me outside.

The Homeporters relate to one another with this hospitality of the heart. Caroline, whose sentences, spoken clearly, never make a bit of sense, can sit down beside Naomi, for instance, or Marietta, and from a distance it would appear that a dialogue is happening. Each tries, more than once, to understand what she is trying to get across. Even if her poor brain has clicked over into paranoiac anger, the reaction is to ease away without pointing out her unbalance.

Marietta is supported, too, by her acceptance of a God of love who oversees her, and all others. While Isaac has no such experience, his base of respect for others prevents his arguments with me from devolving into mudslinging or separation. It enables us to have an ongoing discussion—which it seems is good for both of us.

Mebs and her sisters, Mickey and Helen, and my grandparents lived with that civility. The only solid disagreements I saw between those sisters were at a restaurant where they fought over who would pay the bill. Each wanted the tab.

Some years ago, I found myself in a group of people who seemed to have missed this quality of grace. I could join them in rapid repartee with an edge, but as that pace picked up, I grew more and more uncomfortable. Hurtful things were being said. Down-turned mouths and eyes snapping from some unresolved inside pain created an atmosphere of clowns gone sour. These aren't my people, I thought. There is something to be said for civility, even if a person hasn't exactly lived an examined life. I was grateful for it at Homeport.

"Days Have Turned To Years"

Yearning Just For You

Marietta's daughter, Susan, has married and moved a good distance away, but she comes to see Marietta on her days in the city at a part time job. I am usually at Homeport on those days so I have seen a slow change in Susan.

During the year when I was Marietta's companion at home, I had a lot of judgment about Susan. I felt that her treatment of her mother sometimes edged close to emotional abuse. For instance, there was the evening when Marietta and I were peaceful in front of the television. We heard a door shut and looked up to see Susan. She settled across the coffee table from me and began telling me of the building drama in this family in only slightly coded words.

"I'm really worried about Dad. His blood pressure is up dangerously and so is his PSA. This can't go on." She, the father-loyal child.

"Who is that you are talking about, Sue?" Marietta had been half listening.

"Just a friend…" It was a brush-off. "We are seriously considering a place for her."

She saw that I was watching the movie, and said she'd talk more to me afterwards. Only minutes later she returned with a small nail clipper.

"Mom, your nails are too long. I'm going to cut them."

"Oh no, Susan. They aren't too long. I like them this length." This was the voice of the elegant matron whose closet full of gorgeous dresses attests to the time her husband and she attended Presidential gatherings.

"Shush, shush! Mom, this has to be done."

Marietta was overridden, her hand pulled over into Susan's lap, the nails cut very low. Any protest evoked the same shushing. Marietta looked over at me and rolled her eyes. And again, after Susan huffed about Marietta holding still, Marietta looked at me and made a child's face of untempered disdain: tongue out and down, eyes rolled up.

Nothing else was said until Susan felt the job was done, and got up. Marietta said, "Thank you dear." No touch of irony here? Was the capitulation total?

Susan answered, "You're welcome." Not a hint of her violation?

When I arrived the next day, mother and daughter came in after me, Marietta's hair was cut unbecomingly short, like her nails. Susan said, "I sent (the other caregiver) home because I wanted to be with my Mom."

She left soon afterwards, left me with Marietta, her personal boundaries invaded, hopelessly unsure of herself, afraid and guilty.

This experience landed just a day after I had arrived to find Marietta's husband in a rage of frustration. I felt the charged energy as soon as I entered. "What has happened?" I asked.

"She's hidden very important papers I was to take to the bank today. They were on my stairs to bring down for her signature. I have searched all over but she has secret places where nothing is found." Hank barely contained his rage as Marietta came from her room, her body folded like a puppy expecting punishment.

"You just must not take things away, Marietta. Maybe Lynn will help you find them. I've got to go and cool off."

I took her arm. As we walked into her room, she asked, "What is it he wants?"

"It is a large manila envelope. Let's look for it."

With the luck of an outsider, I opened her magnificent desk, reached in between some books, and pulled out the envelope. "See, here it is dear, no more worry. Let's go out for a walk after you sign whatever it is."

At least an hour later, as we strolled by the Bay, she asked, "Did we find what he wanted?"

Was it the passion of the drama that stayed in her cratermind? I wondered if it wasn't the deadness of all feeling in this house, except exasperation, that added to Marietta's confusion. I saw that her dementia was not the cause of all of Marietta's loneliness. She was outcast here in a field of anger, disappointment, and martyrdom. It seemed that she had "out-witted" both husband and child that I felt was driving them to institutionalize her among strangers and drugs and rigid rules.

As I said, at first, I strongly objected to Marietta being sent away from home. However, I came to believe that she might be happier among strangers who didn't have expectations of her, where there would always be people around her, and she would not have to wander, like a modern day Ophelia, in her prison-castle.

But that was well over a year ago. The move to Homeport had worked perfectly to give Marietta and her family some breathing room. Now that Marietta had her "sister" Eileen and a safe, active environment, she was happier and less a threat to her daughter. In no way do I want to make Susan seem uniquely cruel in this story. Susan and I dialogue here at Homeport when we meet. These talks are always subject to interruption, but I have shared with her my early judgments about her behavior, to which I now find parallels in my own life. As we found no way to settle our feelings directly with our mothers, we leaked our anger. Susan and I discovered we had common experiences. In her case, her mother was a perfectionist who always disapproved of the child in all her messy developmental stages. It was especially difficult during her teen years when she would not live in the fussy clothes Marietta had always chosen for her.

To my mother's combined indifference and disapproval for my not being more of a lady instead of a sloppy world saver, my rebellion took the form of trying to shock her with outrageous statements, expecting no retort. We never took each other on at the same time.

When I was ten, I found my baby book and asked why it was all torn up. "Oh Lynnie, you were so strong at three. I couldn't stop you." What a monster I was! It was one of many such statements that eroded my personal power and made me angry all at once. Feeling impotent is angry making. Mebs' frequent hostile remarks that she tossed out right into my adulthood ("You've never done anything I thought important") came from her impotence and never failed to stop me in my tracks.

It is all too human to displace our hurt and loss onto others, to judge our closest loved ones and ourselves through a veil of concepts we have adopted as youngsters without clear vision. When my half-brother got his parents together fifty years after their divorce, I realized that we never give up on childhood loss. The best Susan and I could do about our mothers was to develop a quiet self-awareness, a non-judgmental inner parent that catches our yearnings before, or even after, they spring out as judgments. Even healthy older parents cannot respond to or solve the childhood perceptions in our minds.

It took me so long to note my mother's diminishing power. Susan had no such blindness. Marietta's disease put Susan in the driver's seat, a place where she sat most uncomfortably, and, most demandingly. What both of us felt, of course, was that universal longing for unconditional love from the key person in our lives.

Luckily for Susan, Marietta has mellowed and most often recognizes her when she comes. She tells her she loves her often, and how pretty she looks, and tells others proudly, "this is my daughter." Even now, even with her mother's slow disappearance, Susan is softened by the words. Never too late to open to love, however it comes.

"Women Do Get Weary"

Grace is a new Homeporter. It is late afternoon and about eight of us are sitting before the television in one of the suites watching a Fred Astaire movie. A new and unschooled aide wheels her into a spot beside me. Grace is relearning to walk after an injury. She is crying now. I take her hand. She shows me her knee. It is badly bruised. Earlier, after our morning gathering, the aide had made her use her walker the whole way back to her room. It was too far and she had fallen on that knee. Now she is disconsolate. All the losses of her life have arisen.

"It's hard to keep letting go, isn't it?" I speak from experience.

"Oh yes. I am so alone." Grace squeezes my hand, face downcast.

"Not quite alone. Your beautiful cat is with you." I love cats and have made it part of my routine to bring her matted white angora out from her room and brush it every few days.

Animals are difficult for the aides who have then to add brushing and feeding and cleaning cat boxes to their chores. Occasionally a pathetic little dog comes attached to a Homeporter who cannot even walk it. The last dog was blind. His mistress was sojourning with us while her caregiver was vacationing. She would circulate among the different suites, not even knowing where her dog was, but often it would be wandering around the big living room, bumping into walls. One of us would have to remember to take it out to a patio and stick it among the flowers until it did its thing. The aides almost revolted while he was there.

But the psychic comfort of petting a loving animal is now an accepted fact at most facilities. At least once a month the SPCA sends in a volunteer with a dog. Most of the residents like to pet and hold them. Occasionally one is frightened of dogs and must be led away to "safety."

Grace nods in agreement—she *does* have her pussycat.

"Look," she says, "She has handed me this hard peach—as if to make up for letting me fall."

I see her aide is listening. Like each of us who work among these special folks, her lesson has begun. I take the peach, say I will put it in the kitchen. We hold hands while Fred and Ginger ripple across the screen. We comment, appreciate. She smiles at me, squeezes my hand, says she hopes I will be here all night with her. I tell her I won't be here all night, but I will be back to check up on her in the morning.

At five, dinner is announced and I get up to leave. She grabs my hand, kisses it, "Thank you so much. You saved my life. I love you."

I am full as I re-enter the "real world."

"There's Gonna Be A Certain Party At The Station, Satin And Lace"

Chattanooga Choo Choo

I didn't know Eileen still had a gentleman caller until the day I was taking the group for yet another walk around the block. As usual, Eileen was on Marietta's arm, squeezing through the door to the lobby at the same moment.

"Hello Eileen. I've come to visit."

We all looked at this sweet-voiced fellow with the round body and nice smile. Eileen was equal to us in not knowing who he was. I introduced myself. He said he was Joe, Eileen's friend for the last eighteen years, and he always visited twice a month.

"Oh Eileen, how nice," said I. "Here, let go of Marietta and go on back with Joe. We'll see you later."

Eileen was signaling like a kid being taken away by a kidnapper. She was not about to go with this stranger.

"That's okay. I'll go into the living room and wait till you get back." Joe took her dismissal with a grain of that old gentility.

At the front door I said, "Eileen, Joe has come to see you. Don't you think you should be with him?"

As if a light snapped on, Eileen's face lit up. "Oh is he here? Well, yes, I do want to be with him."

I led her back to someone who found Joe, and there they were, close together on a couch, when we returned. Joe is ninety-two. He lives alone in an apartment and drives his car to see Eileen faithfully. I never would have believed it! What a sweet romance, fitting Eileen perfectly.

"We used to dance in huge ballrooms all over the Bay area," Joe told me.

Once in Seattle near the Needle I found just such a ballroom. I was warmed by the intimacy of couples whirling and moving together, who had been dancing as one for fifty years. I felt that joy now, seeing these two holding hands, unsevered by the blackness in Eileen's mind.

Life Above Homeport
"And I Know Just How Much I Have Lost"

The Tennessee Waltz

There are more than one hundred apartments on the second, third, and fourth floors above Homeport; more than one hundred senior people to be kept amused. My sorties upstairs were a very mixed experience, bingo games being the pits. There were about ten regulars who took the game so seriously that it was hard for a novice (and I was one in the beginning, never having called bingo before) to enter and dare ask questions that might hold up the call. There was one man among the regulars whom I call Herm. His irrational behavior made me aware that there wasn't such a division between upstairs and down in that building. Herm greeted one or two women he knew and then settled into a silent perusal of each and every bingo card until he selected two. I asked him more than once what he was looking for. Was there some secret to the numbers arranged on a card that made it more likely to win? He didn't answer, but his bingo mates said, with slight grins of embarrassment, that there were some numbers called more often than others.

If I didn't get the cage and number balls set up fast enough and begin promptly, Herm would begin, face down to his cards, "Alright, alright, what are you waiting for, get going?"

It didn't matter if I was trying to settle a newcomer into the game. I was supposed to be going around with the cup to collect the twenty cents a game from each person. And there was only one way to do that—Herm's way. In my inimitable style, I would go back and forth across the table, saying something to each person, until I got to the bottom of the table where Herm always sat in his wheelchair. "What the hell are you doing!" he'd yell, "How do you know you got all the money?"

He would want to count it to make sure. This was a man paying at least $50,000 annually to attend this bingo game. Clearly he had given it some significance that was not apparent.

I sat there twice a week, week after week, doling out the winnings and the endless numbers, asking myself, "Is this my fate forever?" Tired as I got among my Homeport gang, I never asked that question. Except for Caroline's sometimes violent outbursts, I reveled in the gentleness, albeit with stubbornness, that my Homeporters exuded. I know they weren't all so sweet in their past lives and it made me curious about how the personality is affected by dementia. If Herm ever landed in Homeport, would he soften?

My morning job upstairs was to repeat the chair exercises I'd just completed in Homeport. I would arrive to find about ten ladies, perhaps one or two men, sitting in neat lines of chairs or wheelchairs with spaces between, facing my empty chair. They sat without conversation, unless there was a current complaint about the service of the staff or the changed rules about bingo.

"Hello everyone, how are you today?"

Mildred was the most voluble. "Very good. Aren't we lucky to be alive?"

Mildred was a large, heavy-handed faithful whose cheerfulness had a certain rote quality to it. Mildred's life had become a fight against memory loss, a fact she never openly admitted. When a latecomer would attempt to sit in a chair beside her, she would fling her arms out from her shoulders, making the newcomer move the chair if she felt cramped. This daily act annoyed the others who were silently aggressive in their disapproval of Mildred.

I would start with a spiritual message that we had already shared in Homeport, perhaps a rare upbeat newspaper story or a story of mine about the children I used to work with at the Center for Attitudinal Healing. This Center offers groups without cost to families suffering from illness or other traumas in their lives. Its philosophy, taken from A Course in Miracles by its founder, Dr. Gerald Jampolsky, holds that when we let go of fear, only love remains. One of my little group members in the children's program understood that very well. We had a large stand-up doll, which was at the center of our circle, representing a child with an illness. We asked each member of our children's group to say something to that doll that might help it. Julie, an eight-year old with a brain tumor, sat staring with great focus at the doll until the other kids got itchy, asked her what she was doing, why wasn't she talking to the doll? She responded, "I'm doing the best thing for her. I'm beaming love at her."

In my new role as activities person upstairs, I would add a warm story about Homeport, our singing or the art project we were working on, and invite this group to come on down and join us.

"I won't come near that place!" Mildred left no doubts. Neither would the others, but they would never be so blatant as Mildred.

As we neared the end of exercise before lunch, I would wind up asking if anyone had any good news to share. It was usually Mildred who would declare something positive, often the same thing each time. "I have good children, my health is good, it is nice here—who can complain?" But then the anxiety, so familiar to those downstairs, would begin in a repetitious litany, "So now we go to lunch, right? The second floor. And then I go back to my apartment."

After she repeated this five times, her neighbors were rolling their eyes, making hissing sounds, or snapping, "You already asked that!" There seemed to be no compassion or perhaps the same fear that produced this litany, a dread of getting lost, facing the clang of the locked door, as she was moved to Homeport. I was helpless to show them a new way of looking at that world, and often went back downstairs feeling heavy, needing the calm and loving atmosphere they might never know, whether they needed it or not.

For a short time there was one small beam of light. I offered a book review/ writers' group upstairs. One couple newly arrived in the facility and eager to keep their minds alive would drag their neighbors into our little weekly meeting. There were never more than six of us. I would do assiduous preparation of a review of a book from my home collection: short or long fiction, biography, or memoir. I would invite a discussion during my presentation. How hard the wife of this couple tried to draw each person out, get something permanent going!

I approached a woman I knew to be well educated who had lost her sister, her companion of seventy years, since being in this residence. I asked her to attend our discussion, but she politely procrastinated. No matter how much we announced the gatherings, no new folks ever came. It puzzled me and I wondered how much loneliness and self-alienation went on in those little apart/ments, knowing that dementia occurred with greater regularity in people who remained isolated.

"Root, Root, Root For The Home Team"

Take Me Out To the Ball Game

The Homeport Director has taken a risk and bought a regulation size basketball hoop, and two others closer to the ground. On this day, Mark is leading activities with me. We bring the whole gang to this patio. Some remain as grandstanders, but between us we encourage everyone to give basketball a try.

Of course Bill is up first. He tosses the ball. It hits the rim. A second time, the rim. I have him stand a shade back. Up it goes, and right in. Everyone claps. Bill wears a shit-eating grin. And liking the admiration, takes another turn.

Arnold is next. He lucks a ball right in. "Wow Arnold. Now you aren't just The Snapper, but also the Zapper!" He is quietly pleased.

We invite his wife to take a shot. Mark stands under the high basket and as each woman shoots, he slam-dunks it down the hoop. Those needing to sit are given a chance at the lower baskets—all make at least one shot. Our shouts of encouragement and whoops of joy as each toss goes in, reverberate off the walls of this inner courtyard. I hope the folks upstairs are watching. Man, this group is Hot—no flies on them.

"I'll Be Here In Sunshine Or In Shadow"

Danny Boy

There are some golfers among us. Bill is always good for a round at the putting green. Marietta, though it never was her sport, always hooks the balls into one or another of the holes that represent sand traps or holes in one. Surprisingly, Naomi, the silent, plays well. And Gloria, our newest sharpie of eighty-eight, reminds us, "I played daily for thirty years!" as she makes her game.

We are out on the west patio, our afternoon choice, as the rising breeze softens the sun. The golfers will keep playing with my encouragement and nimble chases after the elusive balls. Marietta and I sneak in a game of badminton—a thin reminder of our days on the city tennis courts. She moves even less now than she did then, but her eye is accurate and her swat of the bird deadly. She has removed her straw hat in order to see my birdie coming her way. I feel the familiar tug of love for her, and sadness, as though I am watching a friend disappear into the distance.

Physical games never go for very long. Dizziness or boredom or my inattention will bring it all to a halt. I try then to rally the group in a circle on the benches for a little mental stimulation. Restlessness or closed eyes is a sign that a member of the circle is withdrawing.

"So Esther (who is just about to ask where her daughter is) did you ever take your kids to Coney Island? Or on the Staten Island ferry?" This might work. If I get a yes or no, I expand the conversation to the group. No response from Esther.

"Did you San Franciscans use the ferries in the Bay before the bridges?" Sophie I can count on to give some history and a vignette. I draw others in. Slowly we might get, not exactly a discussion going, more like individual statements that I paste together. Maybe my art is craftiness, if not crafts.

"O'er The Sea Of Memory I'm Drifting Back To You"

The hardest part for me in creating activities is thinking up arts or crafts projects. I am continually impressed with the simple, yet beautiful ideas that emerge from the once-a-week art teacher that result in something concrete. When I first began, I was a coloring maven and nothing else. For years I'd sit before television with new magic markers and coloring books of costumes—always hard to find—where my small sense of design could play itself out. There is something mesmeric in moving one's hand this way and that, keeping within the lines, seeing something harmonious unfold. It is a meditation of a sort. So I was delighted to find a large pad of simple pictures in the Homeport activities room, lots of magic markers, and at least four willing fellow colorists.

"I'll do this one," Marietta said, choosing a picture of a little girl sitting amid flowers in a field. Bill chose a boat in full sail. I helped them select colors, got them going, and the magic of this activity lulled everyone into a peaceful silence. Classical music from the tape deck on the counter behind us added to the mood.

I hadn't connected the pictures with their lives until I took them back to their rooms to hang them. It was then that I remembered the large, bright portrait in Marietta's living room at home: Her daughter at five sitting in the country, absorbed in picking the daisies that totally surrounded her. And there on Bill's wall hung the picture of him in his familiar captain's hat on a large sailboat.

Their memory might not recall the actual moments when those pictures were taken, but somewhere in their cells, subtle as dust on a butterfly's wing, lies the feeling that drew them to the drawings.

"Sleep Will Banish Sorrow"

Goodnight Sweetheart

I didn't witness this love story. My friend whose parents these were told me this tale. It expresses so well my main thesis that the spirit is alive and well even after a person departs.

George could no longer look after Joan, his wife of sixty years. Alzheimer's had decimated her mind and her mobility. He admitted her to a nursing home and came every day at the same time. One of the nurses happened into Joan's room as George and Joan were curled together in her bed for their daily nap. The nurse reported to her superiors who immediately took George aside and told him this could not happen. First they actually said "Sex is not allowed here" and when that became patently absurd, they said he couldn't put his "dirty" outside clothes on the bed sheets.

George, who quietly registered this Puritan tendency in our culture, offered to put a second sheet over his side of the bed, but had no intention of stopping these daily naps—the one thing Joan responded to with recognition. And so they continued in this way until George died while away from his home and from Joan.

Without any noticeable sign from Joan that she was missing her bed companion, she stopped eating for a week. I wonder if his spirit reconnected with hers by week's end when she settled back into this life's routine, until she was freed to soar after him.

"He's A Devil, He's A Devil"

He's a Devil in his Own Home Town

Different facilities have different rules about sexuality among seniors, and especially seniors with mental limitations. In the story about George whose wife lay with dementia and loved being cuddled by him during naptime, the staff reacted without much awareness about the affectional needs of their clientele. Anything that bordered on the sexual put them into a panic. I was glad to know that Homeport had a careful open policy that could include a healthy sexual life between two clearly "of age" people.

At Homeport, Isaac's mischievous comments about sex couldn't hold a candle to the unequivocal lustful urges of Max. He didn't just talk the talk, he wanted to do the act. Max, a lifelong musician, first came to Homeport with some early dementia, but he was gregarious and could hold conversations, albeit they often focussed on his love of women, especially naked ones.

Much to the surprise of the staff, his attentions were well received by a quiet new member of the group, Annie. She also had good command of her mind at that time. They developed a romance. With the consent of both families this was accepted by the staff, who would respect their privacy when they saw the couple drift off to one or other of their rooms.

The sweet romance between Max and Annie went on until Max needed surgery and was taken to a rehabilitation hospital for two months. When he returned Annie had deteriorated mentally, and the families decided that she could no longer make decisions for herself. This was made very clear to Max. So Max, without a partner for his quite driven sexual appetite, is reduced to telling the morning gathering of Homeporters and aides how much he likes looking in the window at the fire station where the fire women dance naked.

"Fill Your Platter And Dig, Dig, Dig Right In"

If I Knew You Were Comin', I'd a Baked a Cake

Someone gets the cockamamie idea for a cooking class for the gang on a day I am in charge. I'd ignored the idea at least once before. I know that most of these people had spent little time in a kitchen. They had cooks or were childless and ate out often. And those who had cooked couldn't care less about preparing their own food now, just serve it hot and on time!

There is no stove or oven in the unit kitchenettes so the idea is to have uncut fruit delivered ahead of the snack time and we will all cut it together. I get wet cloths and wash all the hands.

There are never any sharp knives in Homeport, but suddenly they are sprouting on the table like a police station display after a raid. There is a silver tray upon which the cut fruit will be arranged, and one cutting board that I take charge of, cutting the melons, apples, and bananas into manageable pieces.

Everyone has a knife and paper napkin. The more mentally clear ones help the others. The fruit juice gushes as the activity enters high gear. Marietta cuts out a piece of melon and eats it. She gives another piece to Eileen who does the same. I explain that she is to make nice slices and then we'll put them all together on the silver tray for our snack.

"Why?" says she, plunking in another piece. Postponed gratification makes no sense to her. But others are dropping their pieces of banana or melon or apple onto the tray. Gloria is arranging it. Amazingly, all are having a good time.

Typically, Naomi has wrapped a knife in a napkin and is hanging on to it. I let her keep it while we sing our self-congratulations. I am reminded once again how every person likes to feel helpful, feel he or she is doing something constructive. Later, the knives (even Naomi's) restored to the kitchen, we sit out in the sun for snack time. And the oddly cut pieces of fruit taste especially good. I think of Anne Morrow Lindbergh's wish as an artist, "to see a divinity in what the world deems gross material substance."

"A Little Nest That's Nestled Where The Roses Bloom"

My Blue Heaven

We have a new resident, John, a warm, deep voiced former New Jerseyite whose accent is wonderfully familiar to me. John is a basso and he loves to sing. He loves an audience too, and every time we gather, before the activity begins, out booms John's loud bass in a slightly off-key rendition of a hymn, an aria, or one of the songs from our sing-alongs. John is thrilled to be here. His life sounds like a page from Arthur Miller's <u>Death of a Salesman</u>. Apparently he had spent most of his adult life adrift as salesman. If he'd ever had a wife or family, he never mentioned them. I didn't read his whole record. In any case, he had ended up in a slightly seedy residential hotel where a fellow resident noticed that he wasn't keeping himself clean, and seemed to have lost forward motivation. Here at Homeport, he is one of the more alert residents.

His brash outward appearance is belied by the watchful look he gives at first greeting, as though he expects to be rebuffed. My wild mind first flashed on my mother's 'Johnny-in-the orphan-home' story.

Mabel, (not yet 'Mebs') still soft at ten, but growing tall, has big boned hands and feet. Her family lives in a house owned by the Fort Lee Christian Orphan Home, founded by her parents "to save children from poverty and drink." She and her sisters wear clothes donated by people of good will, so the gift of a gold chain bracelet from a visiting uncle brings giggles of joy. It is evening, after prayers. Her mama speaks. "Mabel, it was nice of Uncle Ivar to give you this bracelet, ya?"

"Oh, yes," she rhapsodizes.

"So you know it is better to give than to receive, ya?"

"Yesss…" Now her joy steps back as she feels what is coming.

"And you know Johnny at the orphan home came without shoes. For the money from this gold he could have his shoes. Wouldn't God want that?"

64

She struggles painfully while her sisters watch, wide-eyed. She knows she has lost her bracelet.

Who can win against God?

John was about the right age and from the area of my grandparents' charity. I never learned his childhood story, but wouldn't that have been perfect to meet him all those years later, knowing his new shoes had been my mother's heart-rung donation?

I chalked up his hesitation to his years as a cold-calling salesman, until I learned that he is one of several low-income people that the for-profit company is required to take only for the length of government subsidies. I feel tender for him because once I was in such a position and there are myriad methods, subtle and unsubtle, that make a poor person feel "less than" in our affluent land.

I love his singing, so I join him and encourage others to add to our chorus. His joy at being so well cared for, perhaps for the first time since he was very young, adds lightness to this place. Homeport, despite our daily small tragedies, or the large ones where we lose a resident to death or a nursing home, is a happy place.

"Lying Here Sighing For One Touch Of Rain"

The Touch of Your Hand

The aim of group games is to give each participant a sense of winning. Bingo is a challenge. Each person has her small board in front of her and enough tiny red plastic disks like the old tiddlywinks I played as a child. I roll the numbers out of the cage, call them, and put them in their slot on my master board. Then I have to look at each board to see that the participants are covering the right ones.

It is this game especially that indicates the slippery slope of a mind in retreat. Marietta one day will be in her own fantasy of how to use her chips, perhaps covering the whole board, or ignoring it altogether and making neat piles of the chips along the side. On another day she is like a regular at the local church bingo game, focussed, determined, missing nothing.

Eileen too can reach the place where she calls 'Bingo' as the line before her fills in. But if she falls into her "helpless girl" rut, she must be given permission to cover a number. Sophie can play like a whiz, if I speak loudly enough. But sometimes she will sit, humped over her card, dozing.

We haven't prizes for bingo, so I develop my own reward. *A winner!* I leap from my chair, run around the table, kiss and hug the winner, and return to call a new game. The whole group smiles. Hugs are pretty precious items, better even than candy kisses.

This reminds me of the day we were sitting scattered about the living room, having a discussion. I don't remember about what, but at one point I say, "Oh that is so touching!"

Isaac, satyr eyes agleam, says, "I want to be touched."

"I'll touch you," said Marietta, sitting across the table from Isaac.

"You *will?* I can't wait." But he remains seated.

"What are you waiting for. Here I am," says Marietta.

Isaac gets up, toddles over next to Marietta.

She takes his hand, smiles. "There, I'm touching you."

"Thank you, I'm so grateful."

I remember a quote of Keats: "A man's (sic) life of any worth is a continual allegory, and very few eyes can see the Mystery of his life." Yet I get glimpses into the Mystery at such moments. And I let myself in on something else. My drivenness to please, to not disappoint, has found a resting place in Homeport. Daily, I see the fruits of my efforts. Daily I make someone happy.

"One Leaf Is Sunshine, The Other Is Rain"

I'm Looking Over A Four-Leaf Clover

Sophie has fallen a few times lately. And she has begun to lose control of her bowels. I find her crying this morning. The aide, a hard-working soul without subtleties, scolded Sophie for getting up without calling her and leaking loose stools all the way into the bathroom.

"I didn't do it on purpose!" Her voice holds hurt and the sense of propriety shattered.

"No of course not," I say. "She isn't angry with you. She's just overworked."

"I wish I could just die. I'm in the way now. I can't be helpful."

"That isn't true, Sophie. I have learned so much from you—how I want to be in my 90s—as sharp and interesting as you are."

I have only temporarily allayed her misery. As I lead her out to the morning's activities I think how deeply our sense of ourselves is entwined with the body that holds our essence within it. Its solidity keeps us grounded, but too frequently it becomes *all*. And most especially when it fails in some way. I am reminded of my friend and mentor, Morrie Schwartz, who managed to rise beyond the body's experience of dying. Slowly choking to death from Lou Gehrig's disease, he brought his essence along with his failing body, mentoring willing students until the very last breath.[1]

He never lost track of his true value to others. But of course, he never lost a piece of his mind. How can one retain a sense of importance when there is no current history with which to bridge the gap between now and the distant past?

---

1. *Tuesdays With Morrie*, Mitch Ablom, Doubleday, 1997

"You've Got The Cutest Little
Baby Face"

Baby Face

Carlotta has visitors. Her former neighbor has come by with her two little girls, six and eight. Nina, the elder of the two, has brought her oh so small violin to play a piece for Carlotta. I get excited and gather a little group to give this child a boost into her career. I call Isaac from his room where he is practicing his viola and he comes along with it in his arm. Much to my horror, before she gets five notes out, Isaac interrupts her to give her some instruction.

"You are playing bumpity bumpity bump," he gestures up and down with his arm. You want to be smooth," his arm waves sideways like a conductor, "don't you?"

He has gotten so close that Nina puts her violin down and goes to her mother for support. But Isaac is back in his lost world where he did know how to help a student, an adult, deepen their playing. He doesn't see what he is doing to this innocent performance. He begins to repeat himself. I try to distract him and he says, "Mind your own business. You don't know anything about music."

Finally, thank goodness, the Director comes along and steps right between Isaac and the child, tells him the lesson is over. He sulks, walks away. I feel terrible. The mother is hugging her child, and it takes awhile before she can convince Nina to play her piece through for Carlotta. She does and we clap. I hope the appreciation takes precedence in her memory.

This is an important lesson for me as caregiver. Isaac always was a moody artist. At Homeport he is aware that he has lost so much and grows very unhappy when he focuses on the loss. I had assumed the small girl with the small violin would charm him. Instead, his tough-teacher self came forth, as he must have been in the past. In this crisis, wanting to save the child from further abuse, I was stymied by Isaac's belligerent determination to bring her into perfection at that moment. I let him bully me. I was caught by my own need to be a good person in Isaac's life.

69

I wouldn't have minded had not the little girl been between us. This was a clear moment when it made the difference to be in a facility where there are enough caregivers who step in cleanly to change a client's focus when a colleague is limited by her own issues.

"But She's Always The Lady, Even In Pantomime"

Strip Polka

Carlotta, close to 90, has little of the demanding queen attitude, which her daughter told me, ruled her growing up. Carlotta lived to act and would go anywhere in the world for a role, stage or screen. Her daughter gave me a list of her movies and I went to the specialty video store for one. I made it an occasion. I drew a group around the screen, saying, "We are going to see Carlotta as a famous actress. Let's see who can spot her first."

Her appearance didn't get the kind of response she might have gotten in the past, but then she, too, barely watched herself on the screen. Her mind could not make the leap. She seemed completely unaware that the person on the screen had any relationship to herself. My try to bring a bit of self-esteem into her life failed.

Though a ghost of her former self, she is fun to talk with because she still has an absurdist view of life, which I share. Today, I see she is alert. She greets me like an old friend. "How are you today?" I ask.

"The worse thing is that I cannot control my own life, take charge." Carlotta has days of vagueness and high anxiety, but it is her failing body she cannot understand. She has terrible scoliosis that shapes her back like the letter S from left hip to right shoulder. Her legs will no longer hold her up, a thing she occasionally forgets, and so she wears a linen restraint that holds her in the chair when sitting up.

"Did you ever imagine yourself as old, with physical handicaps?"

"*No*, never!"

"But you have such memories, you've done so much."

"I'm glad I did it all."

"What do you look back on as best?"

"Love. There was a man—what a mind, a world brain."

"You and he shared a house for a long time. Why didn't you marry?"

"He wasn't daring enough, didn't have the guts I had. There is nothing you can do with your life with someone fearful. You have enough to do to get over your own fear. Many of the men I met didn't have guts."

"Your daughter liked him didn't she?"

"She seemed to. He had my children call him The Giant, but there was no child in him. He did it to puff himself up. He could be sweetly cruel. That brilliant mind could slice off a head with one sentence so the person didn't even know it was gone."

"Whew. But his mind fascinated you?"

"Yes, even so." She pauses, thinking. "It seems to me that most people don't function fully—experience life, accept it, challenge it, breathe it in. They choose to be less aware. When you start thinking about possibilities you are challenged or you get fearful."

"I think what enabled you to go right into it with your eyes wide open is your ability to see the humor in it all."

"Oh yes. Sometimes, right here now, I have to laugh at myself when I am sunk by my life. It is patently absurd."

On another day I say hi to her out in the living room. She signals me over, has something to whisper. I bend over her chair, ready for anything, but not for this story. "See that man over there? Last night he came up to me and told me he was taking me upstairs to bed with him."

"Wow, what did you say?"

"I told him 'you may take someone, but it sure won't be me!'"

"There's A Ghost Of You Within My Haunted Heart"

Haunted Heart

The weather is just right today, no hot sun, no huge breeze, yet warm. Homeporters have great sensitivity to any extremes of temperature, so I am delighted to have time on the patio instead of inside the quite airless core of Homeport. Though the group is assembled, we take time to wait for Henry, our oldest resident at ninety-seven. He is heading my way, being held up by an aide. His baby blues are piercing me as he aims for the chair beside me.

"Hello Henry, nice to have you join us today."

His aide notices his intense staring and says, "He's giving you the eye."

Quick as a stand-up comic, Marietta blurts, "Do you *want* it?"

I have brought out an edition of the movers and shakers of the 20th century. I elect Freud to discuss. "Who knows the name Sigmund Freud?" Slowly a half dozen hands go up.

"He was a famous psychoanalyst," says Isaac, sophisticated musician.

"Naomi, you were a therapist. Did you study Freud's methods?"

Lately it has taken Naomi until afternoon to be willing to come out of herself, be with the group, talk. Now she looks sideways at me and shakes her head.

"But I bet you were influenced by his ideas anyway." I run through some of the terms: superego, transference, repression, using their lives here now as examples. Bill is doing his raging number, fist hitting the bench armrest, face twisted in rage, cursing this blather, this group.

"Bill, you are giving us a perfect example of transference. You are furious at life, but right now you are cursing this place, us. That's a good example of moving feelings from the situation or person who made you angry and putting it on someone or something closer by. I remember doing that with my children. Does anyone remember feeling angry at their husband or wife and yelling at the kids?" A few nods.

Bill can't sit for talk especially if it requires thought. I don't know if he ever could, but not now. He gets up and goes back inside to begin his circling walk the length of the building. I bring out more stories, getting a giggle or two on Freud. I use their present lives, away from all they knew, to discuss feelings they may have put aside, shoveled below the surface. Only the usual two or three fall asleep.

After a snack break I move everyone inside to the activities room where I have laid out pens and paper. "Okay gang, here's what I am asking you to do. We talked about repression, feelings we've held that have never been spoken. Let us pretend someone from your past is sitting right across the table from you. You can talk to him or her. Use the paper and write what you would say to him or her."

I, of course, have to move around the table, telling each person again what I am asking for, getting them going by putting the pen in their hand, asking what person they see in front of them. But most of them dig right in, as if they never had an opportunity to express enough. When they are through I ask if I can read the pieces aloud. Here is what they wrote.

Nancy: (a new resident who is deep down angry that she was not taken care of at home) "There were seven of us. Each of you came to live with me when you were pretty sick. I never thought about it. I always cooked for and fed you as best I could."

Arnold: "Dear Dad, I had always been very close to you, with great respect. All my love, Arnold."

Isaac: "Dad, you were emotionally extreme, even primitive, but when you loved someone you were ready to sacrifice your life."

Gloria: "I want to say I'm sorry for any hurtful thought I have ever had of you. Please forgive me. I have loved you since I was old enough to realize you were Dad—all my knowing life. Thanks for your love and support with my school-work. You did so much to help me. Love you so very much."

Betty (a daily visitor who lives upstairs with an attendant): "Dear Mother, I am still annoyed with you. I remember your saying, 'Molly is a lot prettier than you.' I would never say that to my daughter!"

Marietta: "Henry, I am so glad we had our daughter."

Naomi: "Dear Mother. It's great to see you. I am together."

Jean: (The spunky 90-year old with a teenage figure, to her brother) "Sandy, I think of you very much. I miss riding and sledding with you. Love you always."

Feelings are stirred. I talk to Isaac about his father. "He was pretty crazy, you know. When he didn't think the settlement house would give me a scholarship to study in New York, he threatened to kill himself so I could go on his life insurance. There is so much to think about. I want to write."

Yes, so many stories among these people that will never be told. What will be their legacy to unknown descendants? What is my mother's to me, to my children and grandchildren?

I, too, had a look back to a memory of an important interaction with my mother. One morning, before our last Christmas with my folks in their Florida condo, I woke with a startling revelation. Mom had always given us all foot massages. No fanfare, just some cold cream and a child who sat blissfully while Mebsy worked with ankles, toes, and insteps. We all came to assume that is what she did.

But now I woke to a picture of her permanently swollen ankles from successive falls she had taken. Gallantly, more than once, her foot poking below an ankle cast, she would decorate a tennis sneaker with her large costume earrings for condo cocktail parties. She had never received a foot rub! On the contrary, her feet were often the butt of family jokes about odors and ughies.

For her Christmas present I made up a pretty card: *"To Mebs, the greatest foot massager, for all you have given without return. This is a guarantee of one super foot massage during this holiday."*

We did our usual dance around this intimate role reversal for several days.

"Mom, shall we do it now?"

"Oh no, I have to start dinner" or "No, you go enjoy the beach dear."

I finally asked no more. "Sit there Mom, now is the moment!"

I was flushed with the humility of this act as I lovingly washed, then rubbed my mother's feet. She was beyond making the connection I was making of this experience. I felt old barriers fall and tears mingled silently with the cold cream.

"Adieu, Adieu, I Can No Longer Stay With You"

There's a Tavern In the Town

August 1999, twenty years after Mebs' death, I call dear Aunt Helen to see how she is doing. She is ninety-two and clear as a sanctuary bell. Mebs' other sister, Mickey, is ninety-six, and not so clear. She, too, is slipping into a world in which no one can follow. But she got to her nineties first.

"Lynnie did I ever tell you about Mebs having to give up the love of her life?"

"What! No, Helen, you certainly didn't. What are you talking about?"

"When she was eighteen she met a handsome dark-haired man at one of the parties we went to in our small town. Oh they were a handsome couple—she so fair, he so dark. They were deeply in love."

"And?" I can't learn this fast enough.

"Your Nana, our mother, forbade the marriage."

"Why ever did she, and why ever did that stop Mom?"

"He was a premed student at Harvard, but his father was an Irish Catholic bar owner. You know how Nana hated booze. She saw too many children orphaned from drink. She couldn't allow it."

"And the guy just backed off, and Mom went along with it? And then she turned around and married Dad, a divorcé with kids and a woman-chaser reputation?"

"Yes, she did, and lived to regret it. Poor Mebs, she was so unhappy. Our family talked only once about her situation. Nana even suggested a divorce, can you imagine? Your Dad was having affairs soon after you were born, but Mebs felt she couldn't do a thing. She had you, and his two sons, six and fifteen, and no job she could fall into. We never talked about it again."

I finish the conversation in a hurry. The feelings: Anger at my mother's few choices her whole life; the shock of knowing I have been hanging into false concepts forever…*dear Goddess, all these years I've imagined she didn't love me, that it was some failure of mine, and now I see she was deeply depressed and no one did a thing.*

She never pulled out. It is amazing she lasted as long as she did. The drink numbed, but surely must have added to her depression. My mother suffered her life alone, confiding in no one. I believe it contributed to her dementia and early death at sixty-nine.

Oh my poor mother, how I wish you had told me, how I wish I could have heard you! We could have been sisters together in our shared pain and love. I weep until I feel my heart might burst. *Oh, mama, I had it all wrong.*

I am in so much feeling for the next days that I go over and over what I know of Mebs' life. I really know so little! Unlike Carlotta, who had many men and picked and chose her lovers, Mebs was an innocent. Her strict Lutheran upbringing excluded the vanity of mirrors, yet she became a Flapper in the charged world of the Prohibition Era. Like many of the women of her day, caught by church dictums and the frequent references to "white slavery" bandied about back then, her joy for life and sexuality were compromised by the shame of her woman's body.

If there was pleasure in her sexuality, it was a well-protected secret. Her lost love, the Irish Catholic doctor with the bartending father my grandmother could not forgive, was lover in her mind only. Now I understood it was he to whom she would refer when she was annoyed at my father. "I should have married *him,*" she would mutter, second or third drink in her hand. I said at least once out of ignorance, "But you didn't. Something in you liked the wild man Dad was even then."

Near the end of her life, in the nursing home, I found her propped up on pillows, her comatose roommate nasaling noisily nearby.

"Oh Lynnie, you won't believe what happened last night! My roommate was snoring away, but I was awake, and a priest entered the room. He came over to my bed and scooped me up in his arms without a word and began walking away with me. I told him in no uncertain terms that we knew the Monsignor in our town and we still had a car there. Well, he carried me back to my bed and sneaked off. Isn't that something?"

All these years later I wonder if her story wasn't the result of her disappointment that her Catholic beau didn't fight for her, steal her away.

In the nine months I worked at Homeport, this book gestated and I found, and released, my own mother. I have been back to visit Marietta and the others. The last time I took her out to a service at the cathedral she began humming protectively. The world has become too stimulating for her and she won't go out into it again.

She always knows me on those drop-in visits. "Hello Mary, it is nice to see you." And when leave, "I love you Mary" to which I fervently reply, "I love you too, Marietta."

And I will, even if we never see each other again. She gave me so much: Singing again forevermore, a surprising untapped well of patience within myself, and the release of strong feelings long blocked inside of me. It was this gift, the ability to feel both pain and love so deeply, that enabled me to give to all these dear people, and opened my heart fully to Mebs, my mother.

Elegy to Mebs

Oh Lynnie, last night, a priest
scooped me up to carry me off.
I told him I know the Monsignor in our town
He put me back into bed and was gone.

There *was* once a Catholic boy whom your mother forbade.
Did you, in your dotage, once again let him fade away?

You send out, like Morse code, these demented stories
distracted offerings to your visitor, your only child, me.

Distanced like a scientist, I listen, fascinated
a hidden treasure cache amid the lacunae of your mind.

Nearing the end, still unmendable, this habit of missing
between us, like fragile, cracked china.

Later, a thousand miles from me, you soar off
on the wings of a high fever. No one sees you go.

No one, not husband nor sisters nor I
gather to say *Godspeed, farewell.*
Your ashes mingle, untended, with others.

Now your ghost, unhoused, visits my rooms.

Tobacco smoke pricking my nostrils.
Pungent fumes, hard memories. I cry out

"Free me Momma free me"
until I see it has been me, suspended
waiting still for words of love.

Postscript

It was true that we never held a memorial for Mebs. This continued to weigh on me. When my cousins sent pictures of the garden spot where they had buried the ashes of Mickey and Helen with little headstones, I wept. It came to me that Mebs would like to be there, in some form, and so I wrote this poem, and sent it south, asking my cousin to bury it beside Mickey and Helen. I think Mebs rests in peace now.

Mebs Speaks

Ah, my daughter, today you cried on receiving a picture,
two graves, my sisters lying side by side.

But where am I? My stone is not beside them
as we were throughout our lives.

Twenty-five years ago, when I left this world
on wings of fever, freed and soaring

you weren't there to lay my body in the earth
as my sisters' children have laid theirs.

It is Earth that binds souls together as they fly free.
I see, but cannot reach, my sisters here.

Send this note, my last request, to them where they lie:
"I loved you best of all."

Let these words serve as my dust, among them once again,
so we may touch in Eternity.

APPENDIX

I have added ideas that might help a caregiver of an Alzheimer patient. These are gleaned from my seat-of-the-pants learning on the job, with a touch of the wisdom that I added at Homeport.

Marietta

It seemed important to remain as equal to Marietta as was possible. By that I mean that I rarely thought condescendingly of her "Alzheimer actions." I saw her as my contemporary with a disease rather than as the disease itself. This kept me honest and more patient than I had ever been before with anyone. Rather than settle for the label, I often pushed the boundaries, as when I breached the silence of the family and told her about her ailment and how it affected her and her family. This was a risk. But I felt the pain of her unknowing, of her guilt and confusion about her family's reactions to her behavior, and I believe she understood each time that I had to repeat the story.

Even though Marietta had always been a slightly rigid, proper lady, I found nonsense worked, like dancing her around the living room, or commenting on people or actions we saw on the street in our travels. She then moved past her disease, added her own incisive comment, or giggled in genuine joy. Such moments gave me staying power. I never played with the language, or did things that would make her work too hard mentally. When there was work to do, I gave her a task and we would work along companionably.

Frequently, I was startled to have Marietta bring up an event that happened an hour before, even though she had serious short-term memory loss. There was an emotional content to the past event that found its way past the blocked cells of her mind. While I have no proof, Marietta's humming of the same tune seemed to be an almost conscious defense against the changes in her relationships. She was forthright (when she felt safe) with her family, but didn't push once they had responded. It was then that she hummed the song.

Ongoing rituals are important to keep up as long as possible. I frequently accompanied Marietta to her church. Her deep spirituality never left her. She not only continued to know the church litanies, but more than once her simple words of faith in a loving God brought me back into balance about issues in my own life.

Marietta and Eileen

Like all of us in old age, people with Alzheimer's retain the basic personalities they have always had. Eileen's stance of helpless fem almost hid her competitive self, but it had emerged as a ballroom dancer and turned up again in her determination to hang onto her latest "man," Marietta. It did seem true, though, that people softened (unless touched by a bit of madness) or perhaps it was just that they slowed, had fewer opinions, and relied more on my friendly caring.

We Keep Singing

I cannot emphasize enough the value of music and singing in the life of a person with Alzheimer's (and the rest of us). Working individually with a patient, it helps to know his or her favorite type of music, and let it be background and foreground in daily life.

Sophie

In an Alzheimer unit, or at home, involve family and friends with the daily activities. This may take some education for the more distant ones who think they have lost their loved one to the disease. The tired frontline caregivers will need time away, freed from the daily grind, to keep up with their own lives. Renewed love can spring where they see their loved one responding to old friends with the same familiar humor, irony, and shyness. Regular visits to the unit where the patient resides will keep them alive to the Alzheimer patient and add depth to the institutional routines.

If you have a family member in some sort of group, take the initiative to contribute your talents or your reading aloud ability. You might have a pet to show off, or a grandchild. Any homely event that reminds the patients of their own past can lead to memories. It is so important to keep minds thinking, going up to their edge of possibility and sometimes beyond, seeing new faces, hearing new things—or old familiar ones.

The overworked staff will be most grateful and thereby do a better job. It often turns into a gift for yourself as you get to know the personalities residing behind the often-blank expressions, and, because you come frequently, some will know you and greet you warmly.

Bill

Because Bill reminded me of men in my past, I was most relaxed in my dealings with him. Scratching his back, strolling arm in arm with him up and down the halls and courtyards, talking about his life, highlighting the talks with easy teasing or slightly ribald remarks, gave each of us the familiar gift of memories.

Though I understood from Bill's wife that she had been dealing with his deterioration and loss of friends for ten years, I was still struck with her comment that no old friends came to see him because "he can't hold a conversation." Here we were having laughs and sweet times. I urge all readers to not give up on a person as long as the spirit resides in his/her body.

People entering Alzheimer's disease, do best when sharing together openly in a group. Doing memoirs, as Bill and his wife did, highlight what was important in that person's past. A visual remembrance such as this can serve as a reminder for him of his place in the world. I know there are some people who just don't want to know it is happening to them, but I believe that number is in the minority. Most of us want to stay in charge as long as possible, feel needed, feel our lives weren't a write-off—that we ourselves aren't being written off. The new medical wisdom is for the patient to stay as pro-active as possible throughout the disease or treatment.

Stubbornness as a Value

I know, for a fulltime caregiver, it is hard to see stubbornness raised to an asset. We all get tired and aren't willing to always think of diversionary tactics. But, from an Alzheimer patient's perspective, it is the life force itself that fights to be unique. When a person loses her memory, she loses her personal power. When taken from all that is familiar and put among strangers in a strange environment, a patient will cling to anything that they can make personally theirs. I consider this basic human sense.

I tried to help a person keep that independent ego by getting to know what he or she valued about herself. Sometimes I had to ferret it out because nothing was volunteered. Whenever I sat with a person I would emphasize what made them special. As in the case with Esther, my own ego got in the way. Life is a lot easier for both patient and caregiver if the caregiver takes the time to self-evaluate and let go of her own stubbornly held concepts—the negative side of that word.

Caroline

Caroline's Alzheimer's progression made connection with her a bit like a walk in a war zone. I knew she had been angry and paranoid for a long time, before entering Homeport. But she always looked so delicious in her pink dress suits and perfectly coifed hair, skin matching it all. She drew one in with her piercing blue eyes. Of course the attendants who had to clean and dress her each day faced the most difficult chore. They didn't have the luxury of time to reach her. This is why I recommend that caregivers find respite help as much as possible, starting with outpatient daycare if one is available. Often the major caregiver, especially a spouse, gets into the care giving habit and fails to notice what it is taking out of them—and is denying the patient. As in Marietta's case, the move to a facility was an asset to all involved. See what Caroline's daughter was able to accomplish in sharing love with her mother without the burden of fulltime care.

Arnold, the Snapper

Sometimes, trained as I am in family counseling, I saw how the family dysfunction would affect the actions of an Alzheimer patient. I know no corollary between family dysfunction and this disease, but reactions are more blatant: Marietta's humming or poor-puppy stance, Bill's cursing, Arnold's rage.

In my ideal world, all families would have some reality testing and training in the dynamics of relationship. Young couples seeking marriage would be required to do a professional assessment of the baggage they were about to carry into each other's lives, and get a positive footing in reality—a hurdle to cross together to ensure some skills in handling inevitable challenges. We humans can develop rocket science, but kill off love between ourselves regularly out of ignorance and repressed pain. As parents, we can find ways around our child's "stubbornness" that don't lead to an out and out confrontation where we are no longer the care giving adult.

Clearly there were serious problems between Arnold and his wife, and they lived within the four walls of this supposedly top-of-the-line residence, but all we could do as staff was attempt to deflect Arnold's rage, not find a real solution for it. It felt like band-aiding a serious wound, and we did our best.

Sometimes, as in the case of Isaac and his ex-wife, the healing occurs without outside help.

Homeporters Out Walking

Nature, even the little bit we can find in the city, is another commonality we share. The artistic/intuitive sense seems the last to go in an Alzheimer patient. Walks outside are important to keep each person in touch with the world beyond the narrow bindings of the fading mind. I saw nature as a child on those walks, open to discover the smallest flower or creature to show to my fellow walkers. The huge eucalyptus trees were good for a stop, a look up at their stretch to heaven. I would hug the tree, ask if anyone else wanted to feel the solid energy a tree offers. Not many took me up on that, but just my act was a wake up call for their brains. Sometimes I would find the moon still out. These stops-and-goes broke through the patterns: walking without noticing, as if we were on some mission, instead of an aimless stroll; forgetting the person walking beside us instead of joining him or her in seeing the moon on a sunny day; noticing the rush of cars as we waited at corners. None of us is different in this failure to make contact. Been on a subway lately?

Literature in the Sun

There is a growing production in materials to use with people needing props to memory:

* Multiple Choice questions about events or people in the past
* Descriptions of obvious places where they are asked what geography is being described
*Music and words of old songs/play reading/movies/personal events
*Words that occur in triplicate (i.e. Beethoven, Bach, Brahms) or the start of familiar idioms/ditties/poems
*Pictures of famous scenes/tapes of the voices of past famous folks
*Familiar smells like perfumes and spices, pine and cedar, oilcloth
*Smells that are age appropriate and could elicit stories.

What is important is that at least several people in the group get to speak up. Their being praised for their knowledge creates an energy that holds the group like centrifugal force. Try the Alzheimer's Association for helpful ideas. Other facts that affect an Alzheimer person's behavior, like how depth perception and color perception change in the course of the disease, are important for caregivers to learn.

As the reader can see, I take any advantage to keep alive the patients' brains. We never have in-depth conversation, but feelings are stirred, memories brought forth. Out of these I find a way to praise or admire someone's wit or memory. I am always stunned at the irony, the recognition of life's absurdity.

A Homeport Prom

Marietta was an athlete and active all her life. Everyone isn't athletic, but most people have done some sort of dancing. Combined with the familiar big band music, it was a good activity that enlivened our small group.

It is hard to keep folks exercising. Except for the walks, Marietta began to sit and count but not move during the morning chair exercise. If I had had more time, I would have hiked with her more, and with some others like Bill whose restlessness needed it. Physical movement affects mood and releases negativity. Keeping a patient going in comfortable activity is best.

I See Myself as Marietta's Daughter

Working with Marietta and the Homeport family educated me over and over about the judgments we all make about others and ourselves; the often hidden aches we are still trying to assuage with our loved ones. I learned that, despite having Alzheimer disease, patients had very human responses to misguided abuses of their personal power.

When I thought about the long experience of my mother's dying, I saw some life affirming attributes a care giver needs to benefit herself, and the patient:

*Humor, even amid the heavier moments, which I had with Dad and my aunts.

*Keeping the brain exercised, being present, but having a dream of my own and heading toward it, staying flexible to necessary changes.

*The vital element above all others is to find a sacred pathway, an "observer light," awareness that is above the drama. This vision of grace can be reached through some spiritual practice, like meditation or yoga, or meeting with a spiritual counselor. Over and over, I have had to learn that I am being carried and cared for. I have learned to note even the smallest gifts, like a day with few glitches, and I express gratitude's silently or in my journal. As I have learned from Vipassana Buddhism, accept 'what is' at this moment. Being creative with that truth has freed me from my drivenness, my disappointments.

A Visit With Freud

This was a big bite. Freud is hardly clear to most folks. Yet, by weaving here and now events into the terms, my clients were able to grab the concept emotionally. Emotions and intuition hover for a very long time. What a rich harvest I reaped that day! Much more could have been done with each person, but psychological freeing isn't the goal of an Alzheimer unit. Given a larger view, is there ever a cut-off point to the clearing of relationships?

Elizabeth Ochs, a San Francisco nurse, in a First Person article in Sunday SF Chronicle entitled "Get Well Soon":

"In our quick-fix culture, if we can't find an instant cure for suffering, we tend to throw our hands up in despair. But some ailments are best eased at a leisurely pace. I currently care for infants, and their crying, which is more difficult to ignore (than an adult's call for help), inspires creativity. When one of the babies cries, we try one thing after another. *Is she hungry? Wet? Cold? Hot? Lonely? Tired of being on her back? In pain?* When nothing else works, we wrap the baby up and walk in the hall, holding her. Above all, we stay with her. You can't tell a baby, 'There's nothing I can do' and walk away. Why is it all right to say this to an adult? There is invariably at least one thing you can do: Stay there. Sit and listen as someone cries. Stroke someone's arm, hold their hand, and acknowledge your sorrow at their suffering. Say, "I'm sorry you're feeling bad." Don't walk away.

Alzheimer/Dementia Data and Support

National Alzheimer's Assn. 1-800-272-3900   Internet: www.alz.org

Local chapters everywhere   E-mail: info@alz.org

On the web, under Alzheimer's disease or Amazon.com
The reference librarian in any medium or large size community is invaluable in finding exactly what you seek, if it exists.
Public Policy: The National Conference of State Legislatures
      444 North Capitol Street, NW. Ste 515
      Washington, D.C. 20001

What We Know and Don't Know About Dementia

Causes of Dementia

Alzheimer's: 56%   Brain Injury: 4%

Vascular causes or Multi-Infarct (multiple
brain strokes): 14%

Multiple Causes: 12%

Parkinson's: 8%   Other Causes: 6%

Obviously there is still no clear indication of what is causing all dementia. Some dementia related to depression, drug interaction, thyroid and other problems, <u>may be reversible if detected early.</u>

Alzheimer's, named for Alois Alzheimer who "discovered" the disease in 1907, while the largest purported cause of dementia, is still relatively mysterious. It is not clear if it runs in families, and is therefore genetic, or possibly environmental. Scientists are still not certain what causes this disease. They are focussing on Chromosome 19 in later cases, but rarer forms that strike people in their 30s and 40s seem to be related to Chromosomes 1, 14, 21.

What seems to be the difference between Alzheimer's and normal age-related memory difficulties?

Activity	Alz.Patient	Others
forgets	whole experiences	parts of experiences
remembers later	rarely	often
can follow written/spoken direction	gradually unable	usually able
can use notes	gradually unable	usually able
can care for self	gradually unable	usually able

Alzheimer's is called a disease of the brain that causes a steady decline in memory, which then results in loss of intellectual functions (thinking, remembering and reasoning) severe enough to affect everyday life. It begins gradually, causing a person to forget recent events and to have difficulty performing familiar tasks. The advance of the disease varies with each person. Confusion, personality and behavior changes, and impaired judgment result. Communication becomes difficult as the person with Alzheimer's struggles to find words, finish thoughts, or follow directions. Eventually a person with this disease becomes totally unable to care for herself. Death occurs generally between 8 and 20 years.

One out of ten citizens over sixty-five and a higher percentage over eighty-five will suffer from Alzheimer's disease. Currently there are over four and a half million affected. Family members and other caregivers are treating three million of those at home. Without a slow down of this disease, this population is expected to double: twenty-two million worldwide will be affected by 2025.

Scientists at the Stockholm Gerontology Research Center, Karolinska Institute in Sweden in an article in Lancet medical journal found that the more socially isolated older folks were, the more likely they were to develop dementia. They asked 1,200 people ages seventy-five or older whether they lived alone and had friends, and what was the quality of rapport with their children. They were monitored for three years and those who lacked a social network were 60% more likely to develop dementia.

Bibliography

Only a few of the many books out today:

1. <u>There's Still a Person in There: The Complete Guide to Preventing, Treating, and Coping with Alzheimer's Disease</u>, Michael Castleman, co-author, Putnam, 1999.

2. <u>The 36-hour Day</u>, revised edition, Nancy L Mace and Peter V. Rabins, Johns Hopkins University Press, 1991. This has a huge bibliography and resources list.

3. <u>Elegy for Iris</u> by her husband, John Bayley. The story of Iris Murdoch's sink into dementia and his loving care. G.K. Hall, Maine

4. <u>Wilfrid Gordon McDonald Partridge</u>, a children's book for adults too, by Mem Fox, illustrated by Julie Vivas, Kane/Miller Book Publishers, P.O. Box 529, Brooklyn N.Y 11231, or most bookstores.

5. Two videotapes taken by children with their Alzheimer patient parents are excellent:
   > *Complaints of a Dutiful Daughter* by Deborah Hoffmann, 1995: Women Movies, 212-925-0606

   > *Pop* by Joel Meyerowitz, WGBH, Boston.

About the Author

Lynn Scott, Ed.M. Harvard School of Education, has had careers that circled around people: therapist, group facilitator, mediator, and companion to seniors. She has been reforming her learning into writing since 1987. She contributed to an updated version of *Our Bodies, Ourselves,* and to *Ourselves Growing Older,* and to two anthologies. She won first prize for fiction and poetry, and a second for her chapter on Marietta at the Jack London Conference of the California Writers' Club. Her poems appeared in the Spring and Fall Quarterlies of the California State Poetry Society and in *Poetalk*; four poems about her experience with breast cancer appeared on the web site of The Western Journal of Medicine. Her next book is a collection of fictional stories about unique characters in a small San Francisco neighborhood.

Web site: www.lynnscottbooks.com

978-0-595-36211-0
0-595-36211-7

Printed in the United States
40039LVS00005B/388-513